ISBN-13: 978-1-4234-5180-8
ISBN-10: 1-4234-5180-5

7777 W. BLUEMOUND RD. P.O. BOX 13819 MILWAUKEE, WI 53213

Visit Hal Leonard Online at
www.halleonard.com

Be Careful With a Fool

Words and Music by B.B. King and Joe Bihari

*Chords implied by bass.

*Play "behind the beat" slightly.

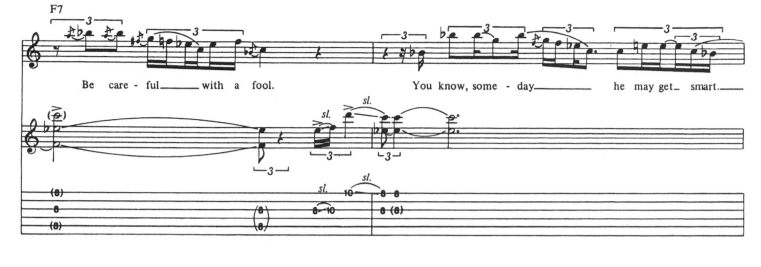

Be care - ful____ with a fool. You know, some - day____ he may get_ smart.

*T = thumb.

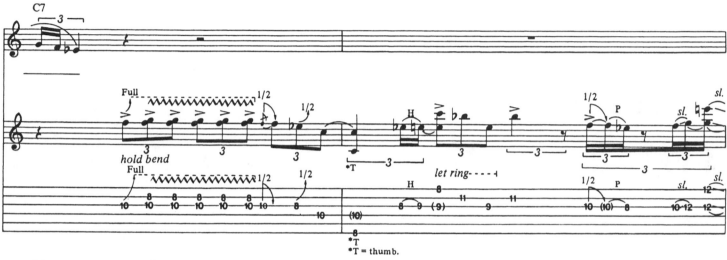

He will treat you so cool and chil - ly till he will hurt you____ to your heart.

*Play "behind the beat" slightly.

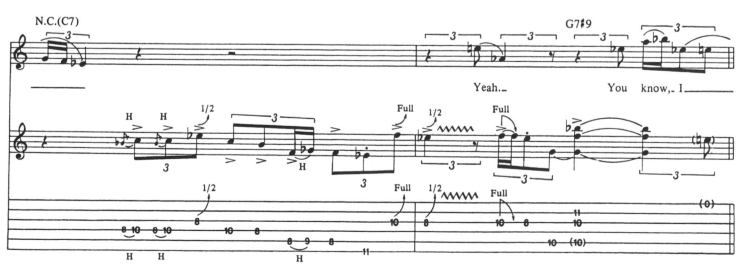

Yeah._ You know,_ I____

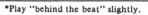

2nd Verse

hate to re-mem-ber,— oh,— what a fool I used to be,— ha, ha!

Man,— I— hate to re-mem-ber———

how fool-ish——— I used to be.

The way I used to love you, ba-by,—

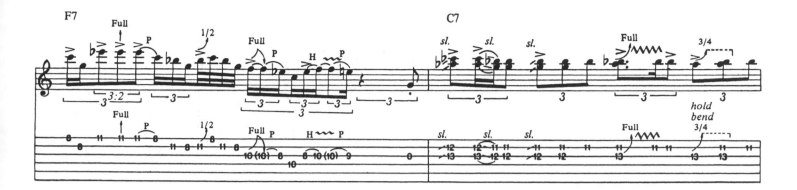

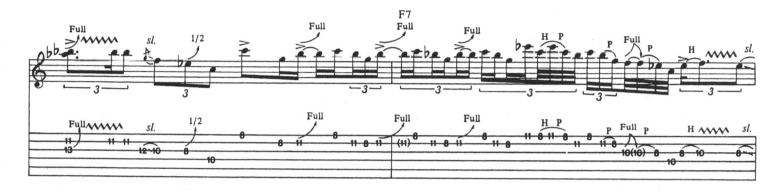

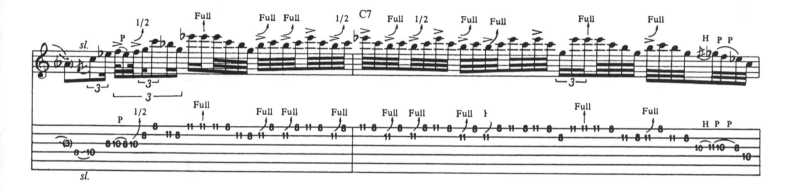

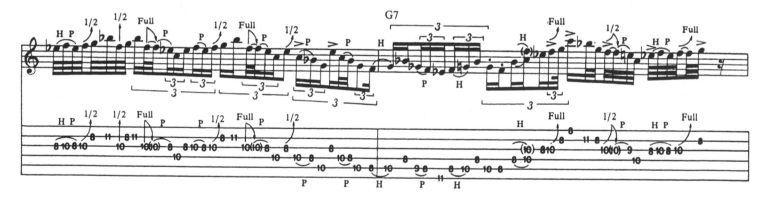

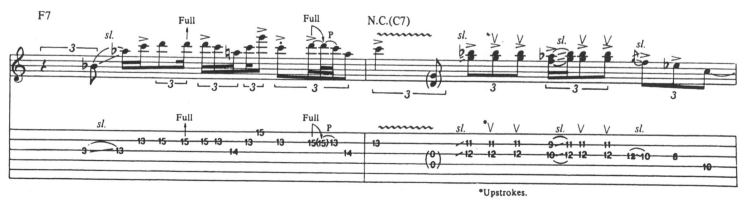

*Upstrokes.

9

*Play "behind the beat" slightly.

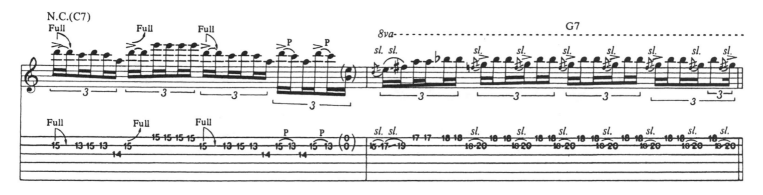

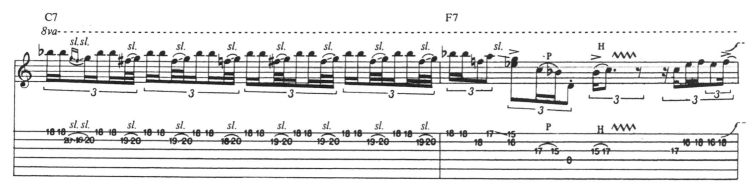

*Play "behind the beat".

*Slightly behind 10th fret.

*Play "behind the beat" slightly.

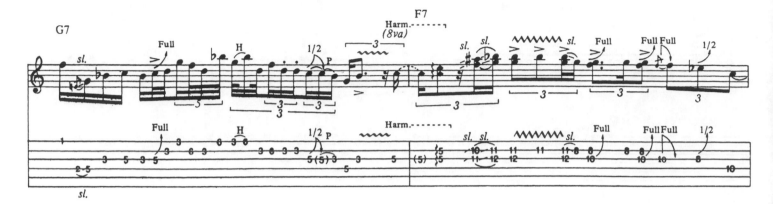

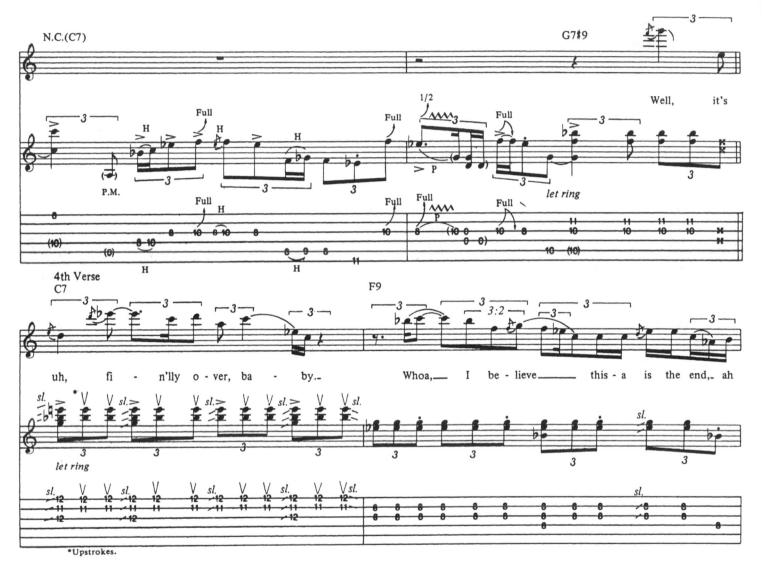

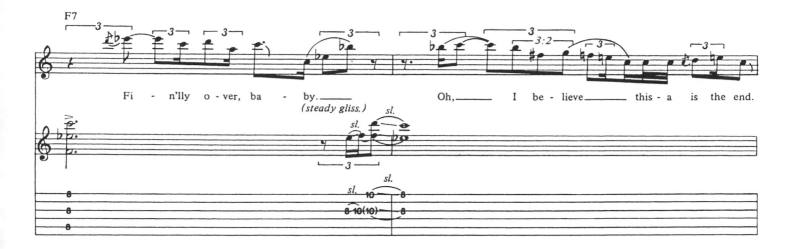

Fi - n'lly o - ver, ba - by. *(steady gliss.)* Oh,___ I be - lieve___ this - a is the end.

Ah! I

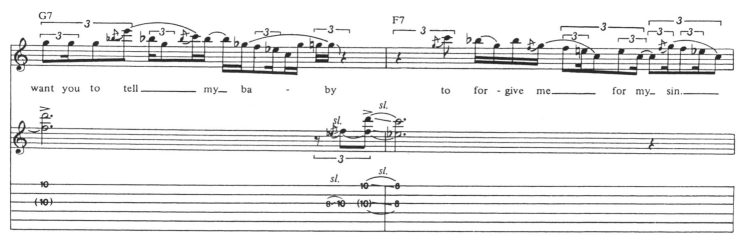

want you to tell___ my ba - by to for - give me___ for my_ sin.___

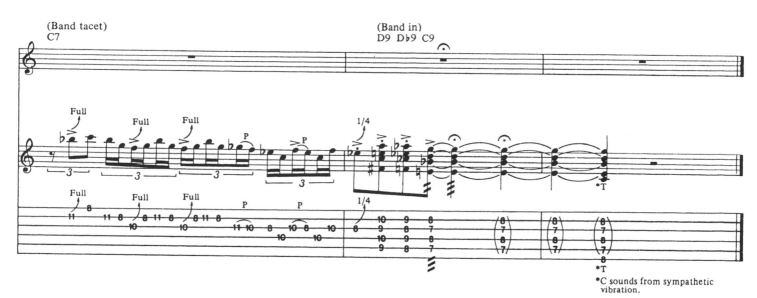

*C sounds from sympathetic vibration.

Big City

By James Solberg and Luther Allison

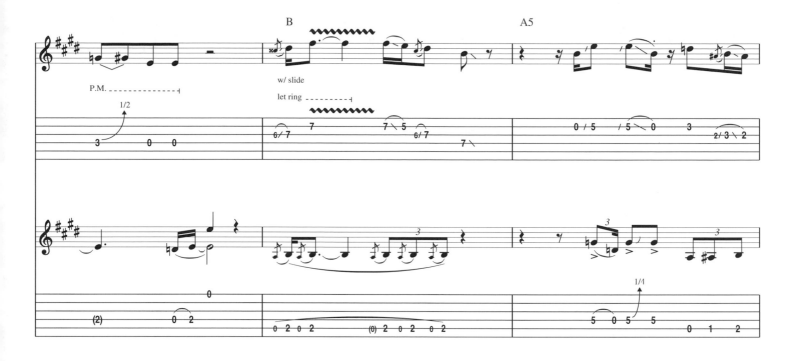

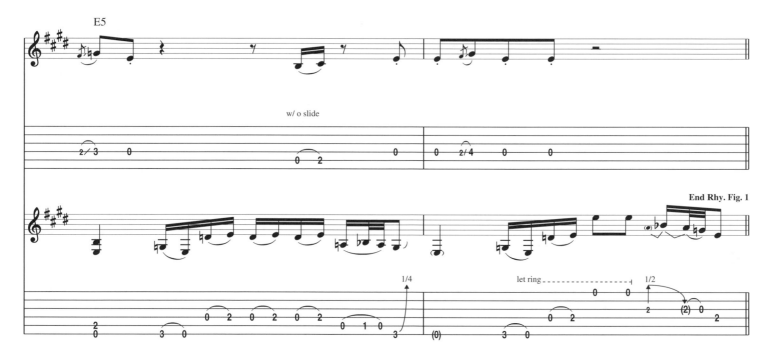

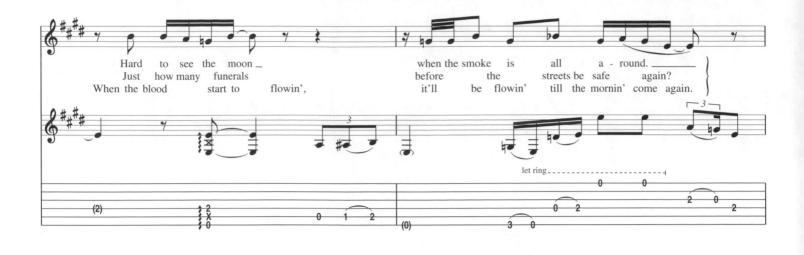

Hard to see the moon ___ when the smoke is all a - round. ___
Just how many funerals before the streets be safe again?
When the blood start to flowin', it'll be flowin' till the mornin' come again.

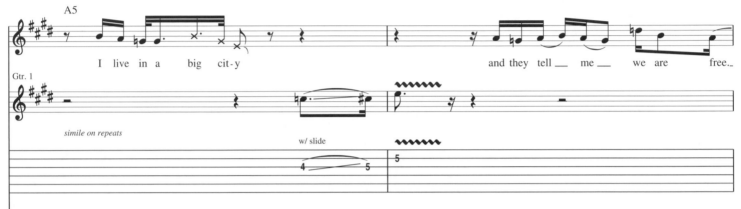

A5

I live in a big cit-y and they tell ___ me ___ we are free. ___

Gtr. 1

simile on repeats

w/ slide

Gtr. 2

let ring

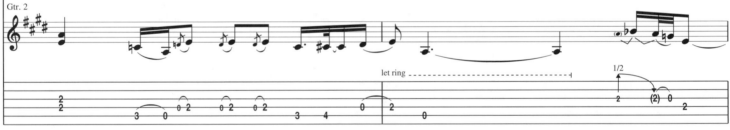

E5

I hear

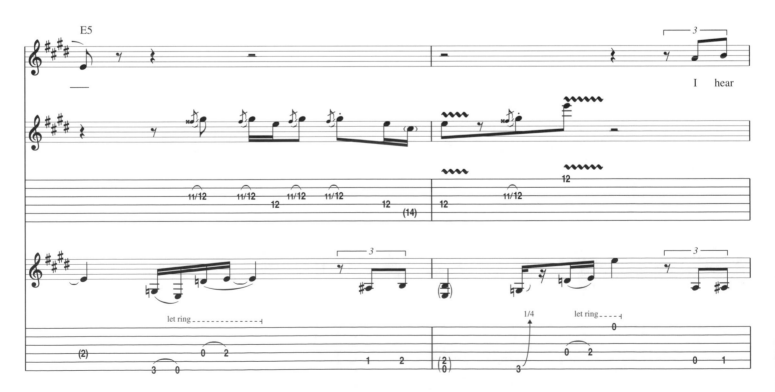

let ring

ba - bies cry - in'; there be ___ kill - in' _____ in ___

___ these streets.

Guitar Solo

Gtr. 2: w/ Rhy. Fig. 1, 2 times, simile

Gtr. 1

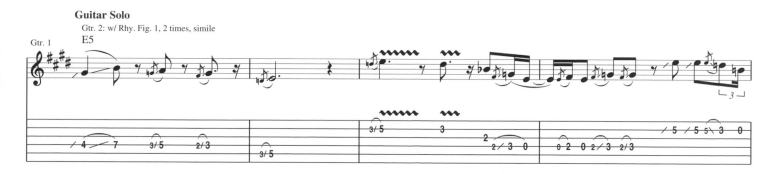

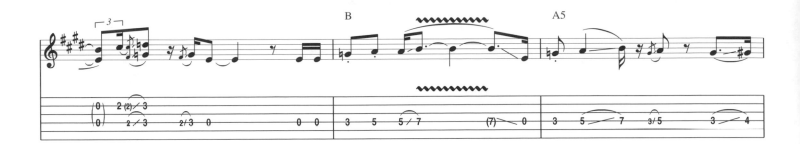

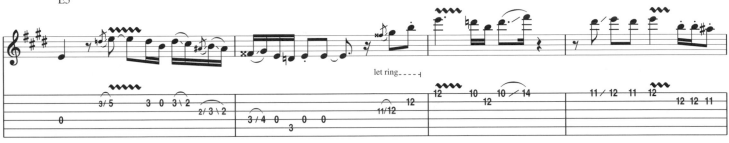

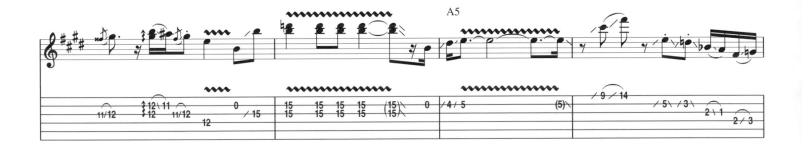

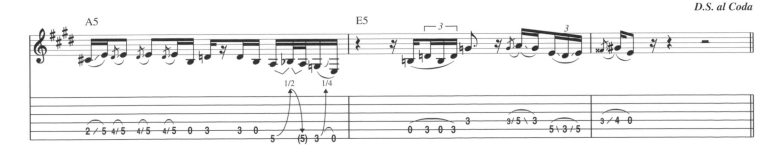

$\oplus$ *Coda*

do you know what that's__ do-in' to me?__

Outro-Guitar Solo

You know it's __ time to hol-ler fire. _____

3rd time, Begin Fade

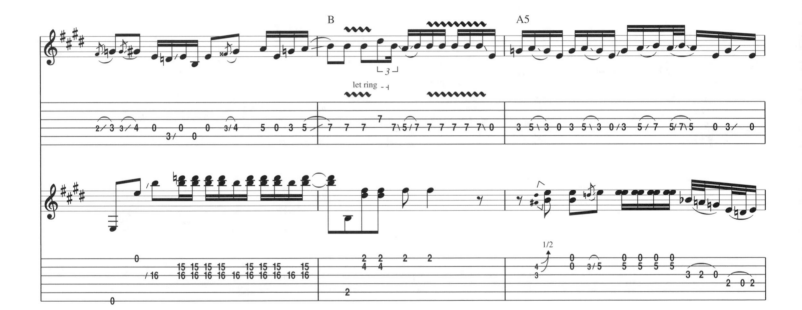

Boomerang

Written by Lonnie Brooks

*Chord symbol reflects implied tonality

To Coda ⊕

* Chord symbol reflects implied tonality

Guitar Solo

Gtr. 2 w/ Rhy. Fig. 1, 2 times

*Chord symbols reflect implied tonality

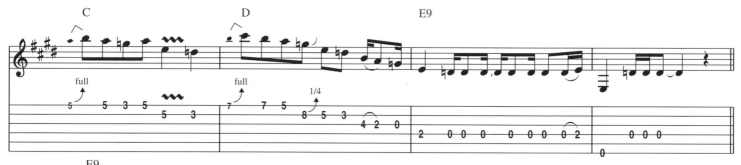

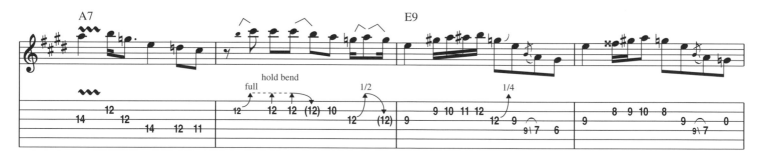

D.S. al Coda

23

*Chord symbol reflects implied tonality

Gtr. 1 tacet

Catfish Blues

Words and Music by Robert Petway

Tune Down 1/2 Step:

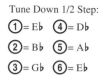

① = Eb ④ = Db

② = Bb ⑤ = Ab

③ = Gb ⑥ = Eb

Intro
Slowly ♩. = 66
Freely

* semi-harm achieved by partially muting between 2nd and 3rd frets

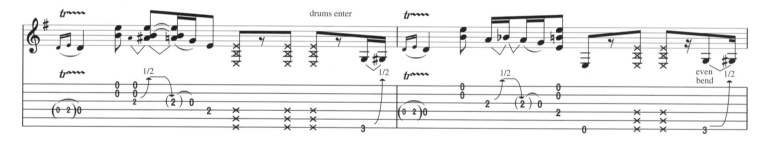

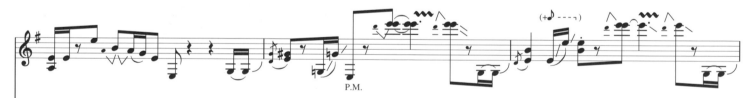

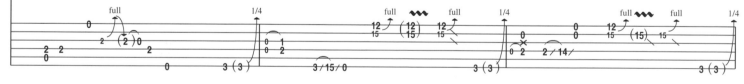

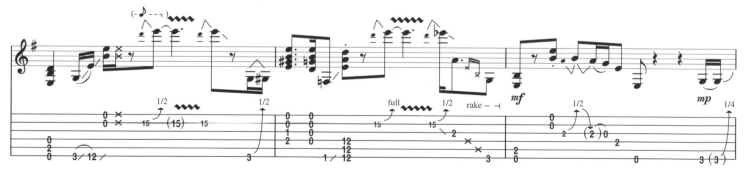

fish - in' __ af - ter me, __ yeah! Oh yeah!

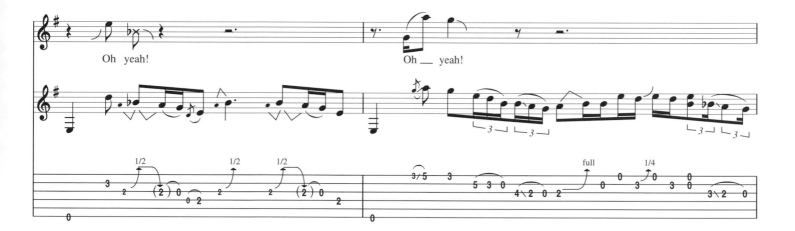

Oh yeah! Oh __ yeah!

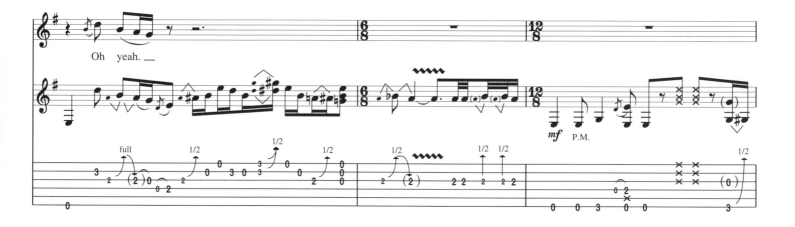

Oh yeah. __

Yeah! 2. Well, now I went down

Verse

my __ girl - friend's house, __ an' I

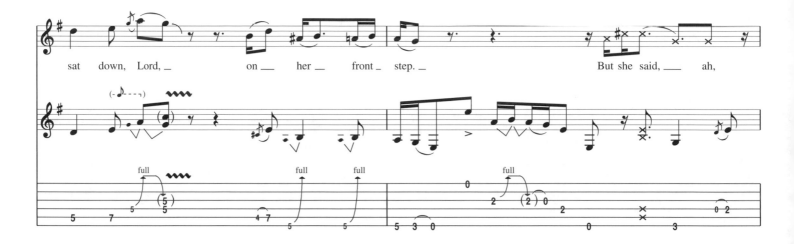

sat down, Lord, __ on __ her __ front __ step. __ But she said, ___ ah,

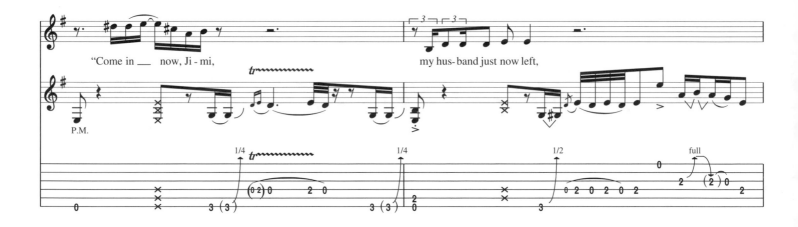

"Come in __ now, Ji - mi, my hus-band just now left,

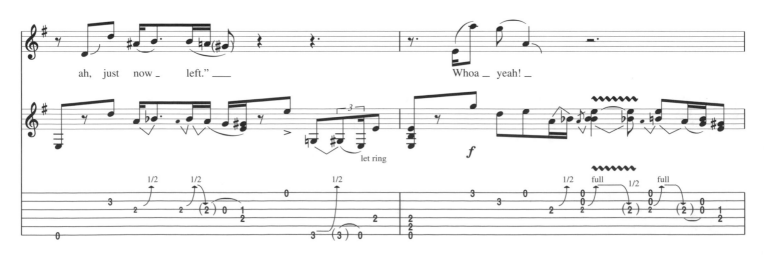

ah, just now __ left." ___ Whoa __ yeah!

Oh, __ yeah! __   Oh   yeah!

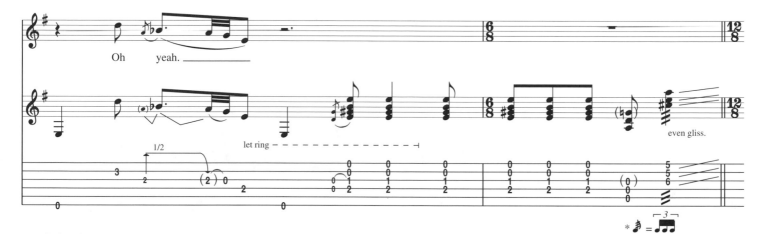

Oh   yeah. __

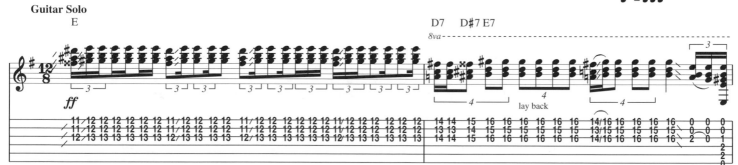

Guitar Solo

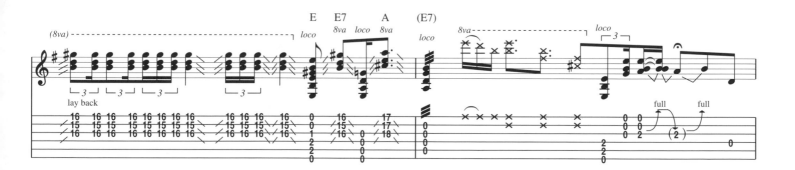

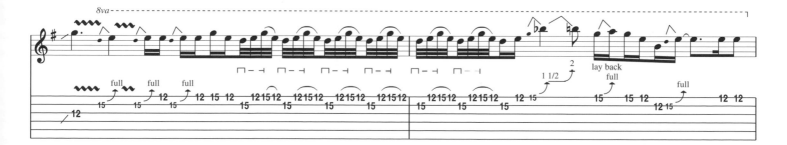

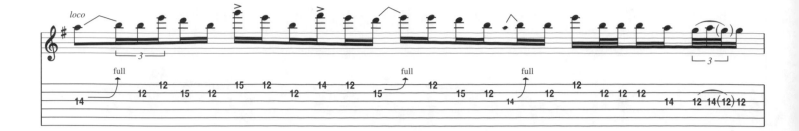

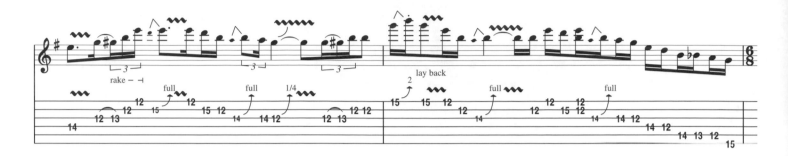

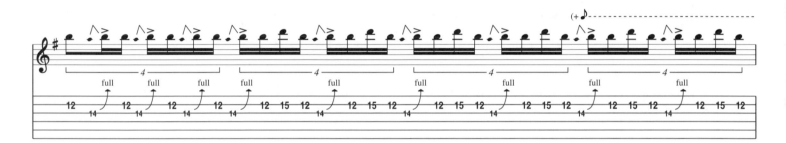

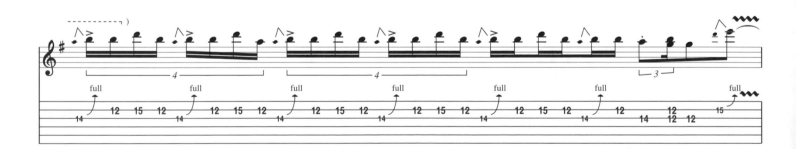

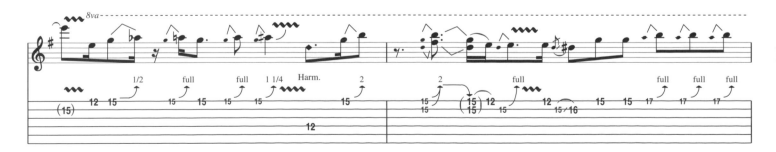

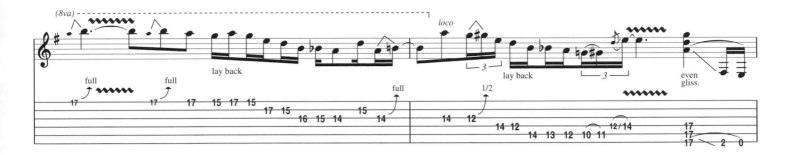

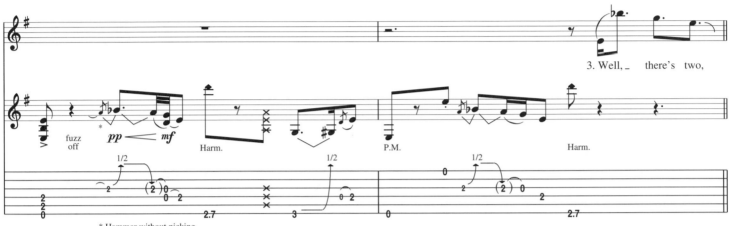

* Hammer without picking

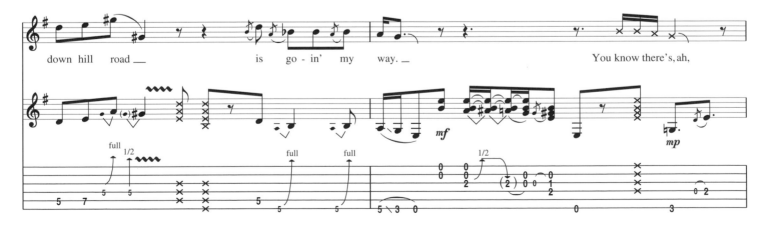

one _ train run at mid - night, _   oth - er one leave just _ 'fore day, _

leave _ just _ 'fore day. _____   Oh well.

Oh well.   Oh yeah

Oh _ yeah. _

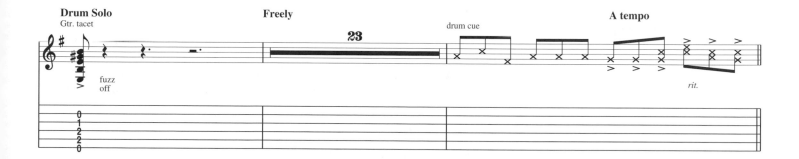

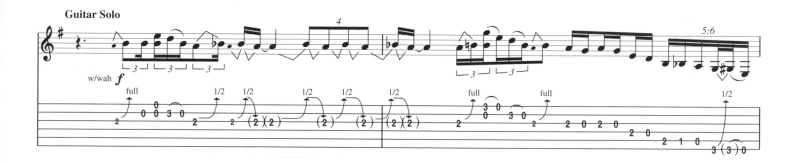

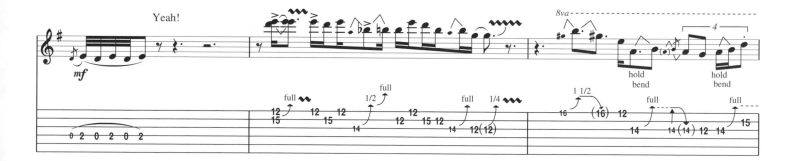

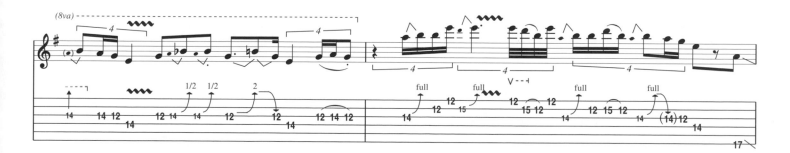

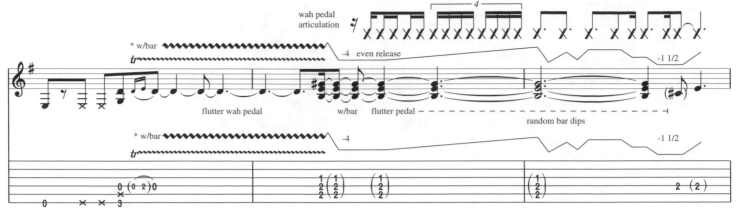

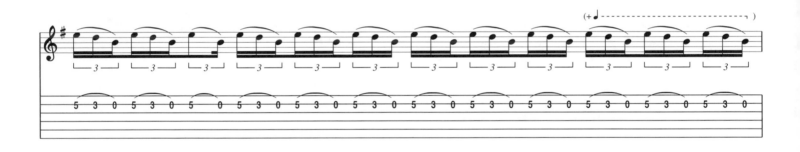

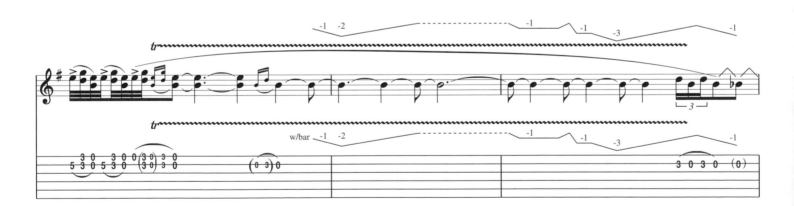

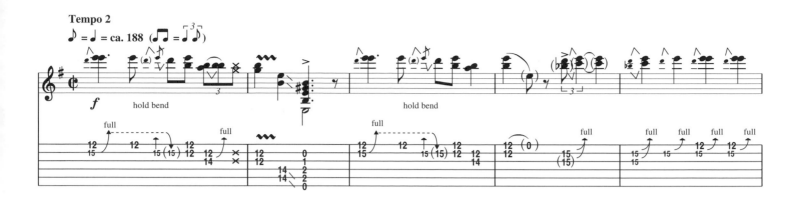

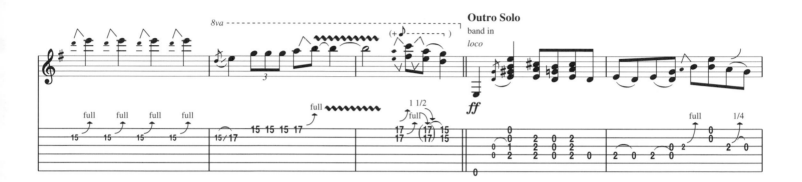

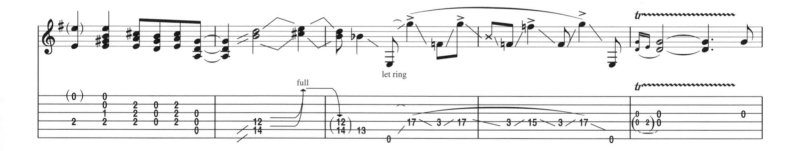

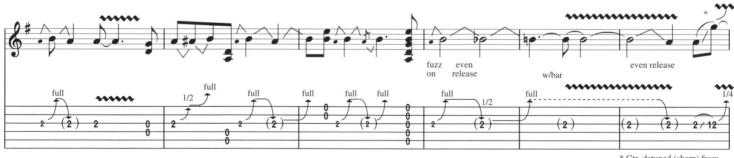

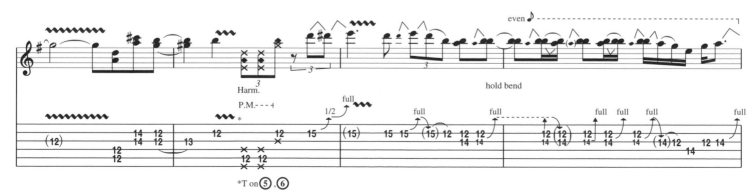

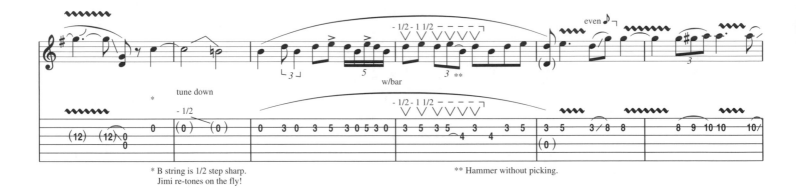

* B string is 1/2 step sharp.
Jimi re-tones on the fly!

** Hammer without picking.

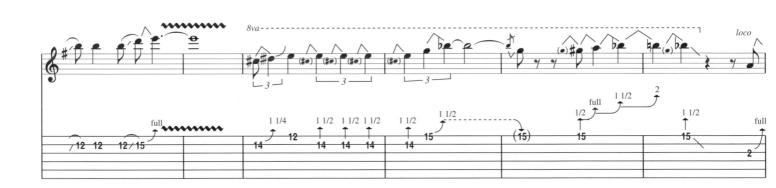

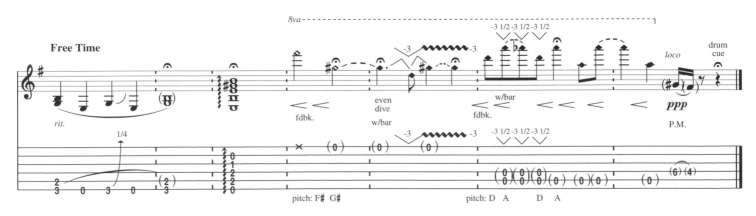

Collins' Mix

By Albert Collins

Em Tuning, Capo VIII

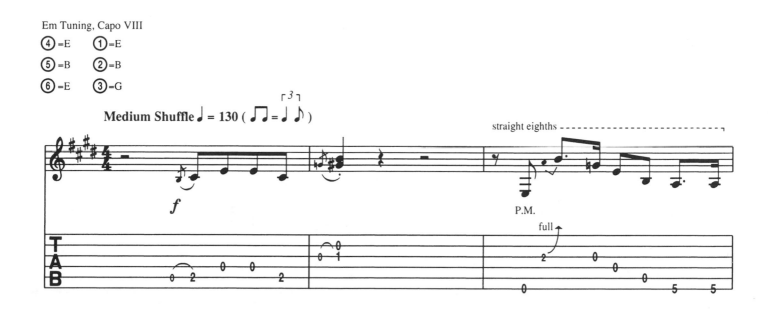

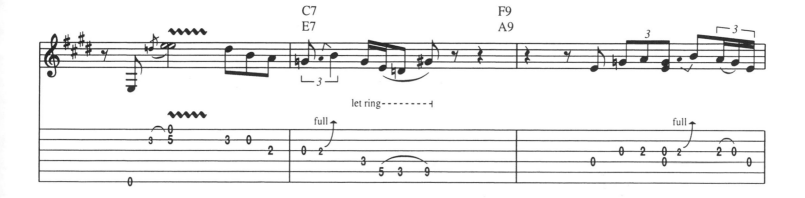

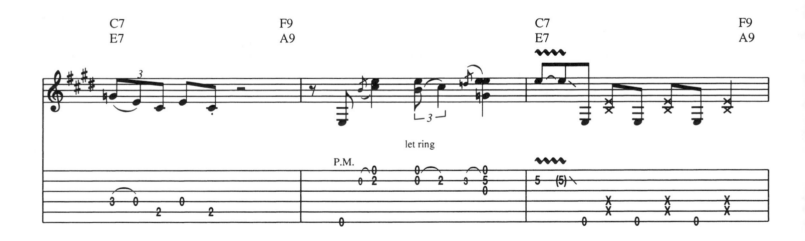

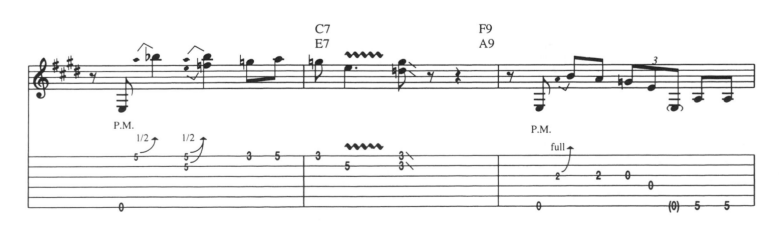

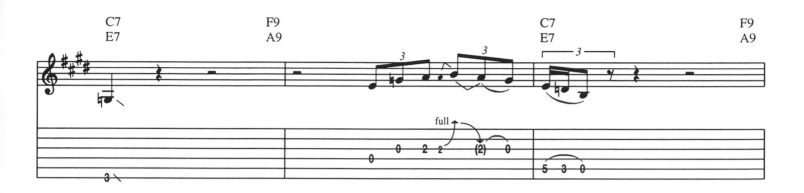

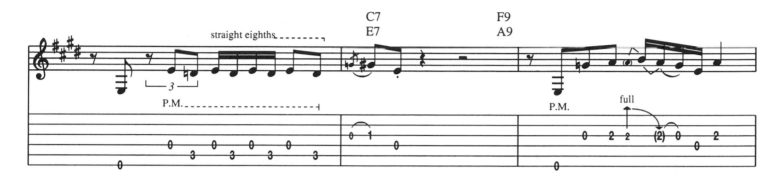

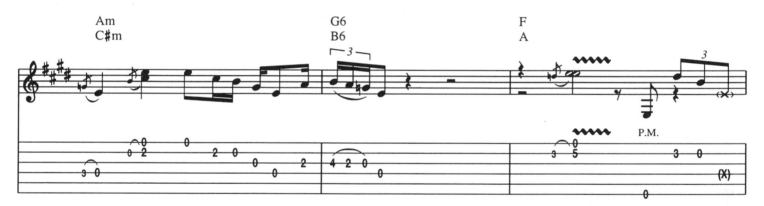

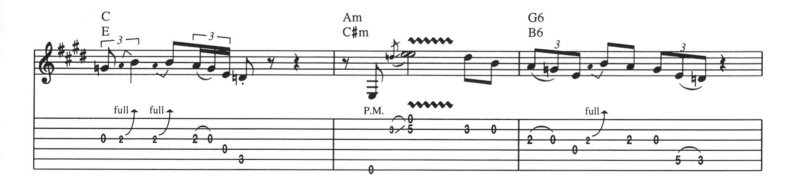

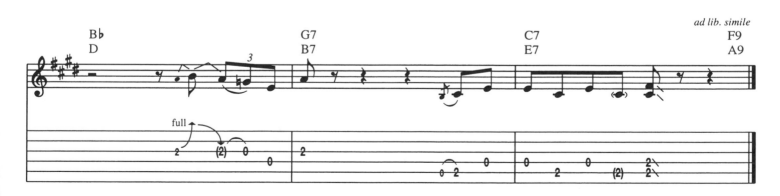

Cross Road Blues
(Crossroads)

Words and Music by Robert Johnson

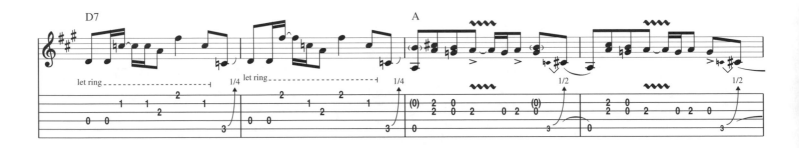

*Chord symbols reflect overall tonality throughout.

to the cross - roads fell down on my knee.
to the cross - road, tried to flag a ride.
down to Rose-dale take my rid - er by my side. No -

P.M.

Asked the Lord a-bove for mer-cy, "Take me if you please."
bod-y seemed to know me, ev - 'ry-bod - y passed me by.
still bar - rel house ba - by,

2. I
3. Well I'm

P.M.

*T = Thumb

To Coda ⊕

Guitar Solo

3.

on the riv - er side.

P.M.

mf   f

let ring

full   full

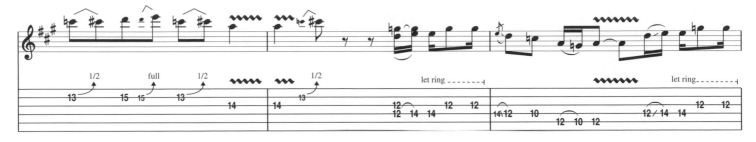

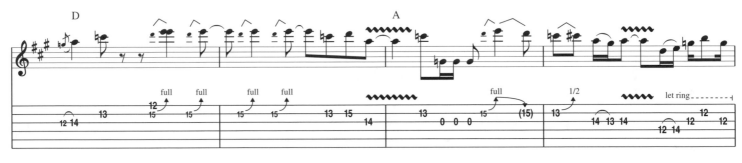

D.S. al Coda
(3rd Verse, 3rd ending)

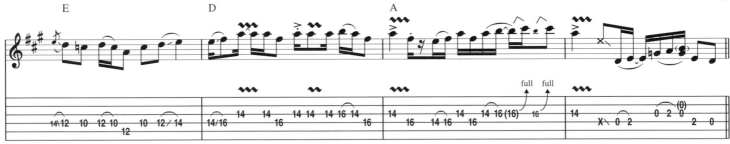

$\oplus$ *Coda*

Guitar Solo

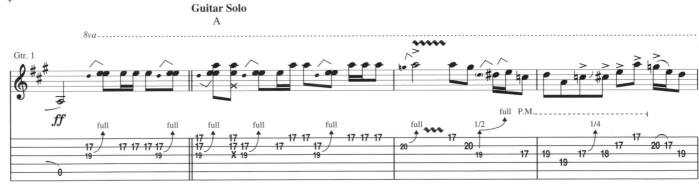

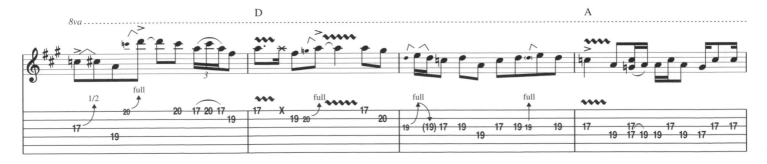

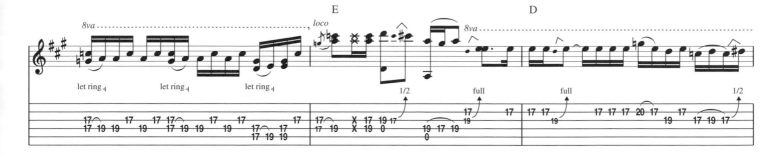

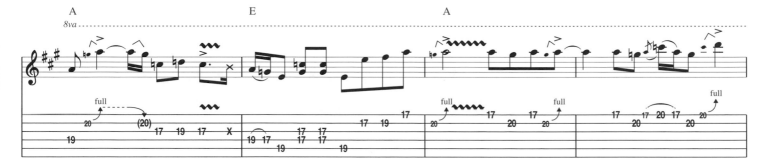

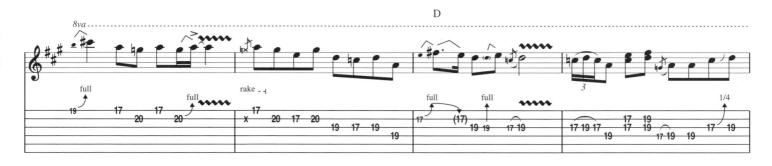

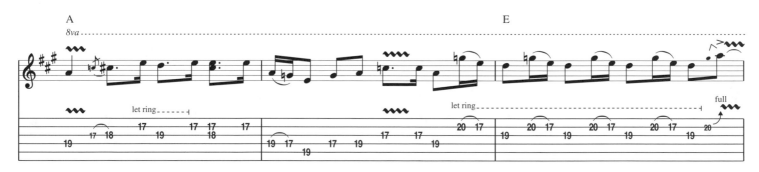

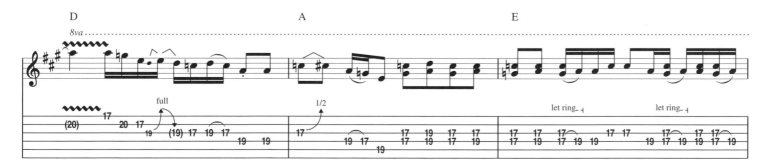

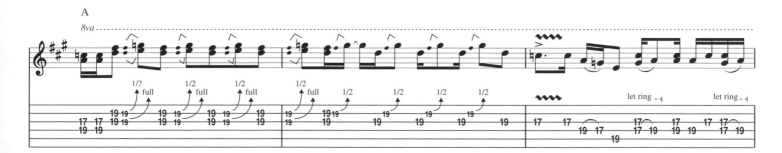

Outro-Verse

5. You can run, you can run,

tell my friend, boy, Wil-lie Brown. ___ Run ___ you can run, ___

tell my friend boy, Wil-lie Brown. ___ And I'm stand-in' at the cross - road, be -

Free Time

lieve I'm sink - in' down.

Easy Baby

Written by Willie Dixon

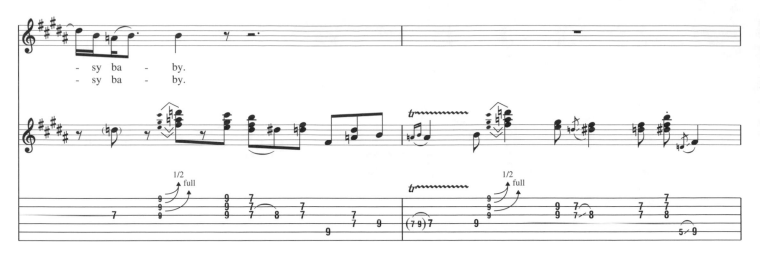

-sy ba - by.
-sy ba - by.

Ea - sy ba - by, _____ won't you love ___ me _____ night
Ea - sy ba - by, let Dad - dy love you night

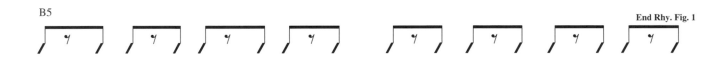

and day. _____
and day.

1. Now
3. Now

End Rhy. Fig. 1

End Rhy. Fig. 2

Verse

you don't have _ to _ work all _____ day.
you don't have _ to ____ treat me _____ right. Just
you don't have _ to ____ treat me _____ right. Just

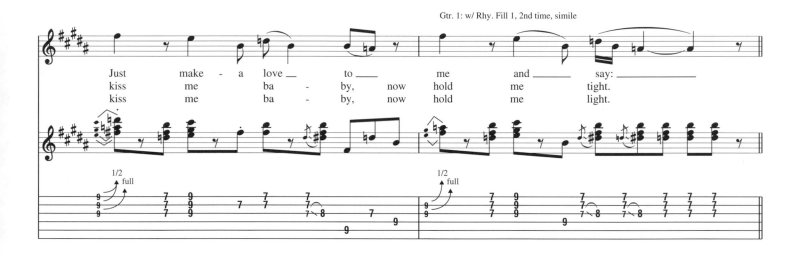

Just make - a love _ to ____ me and _____ say: _____
kiss me ba - by, now hold me tight.
kiss me ba - by, now hold me light.

Chorus

Ea - sy ba - by, mmm, _____ hmm. Ea - sy ba - by. Mmm. _
Ea - sy ba - by, mmm, hmm. Ea - sy ba - by.
Ea - sy ba - by, mmm, hmm. Ea - sy ba - by.

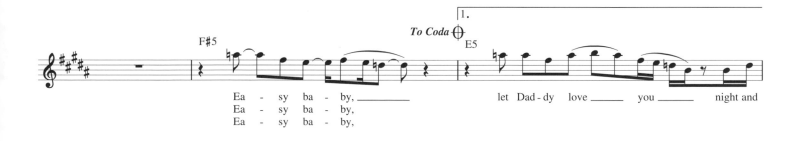

Ea - sy ba - by, let Dad - dy love ____ you ____ night and
Ea - sy ba - by,
Ea - sy ba - by,

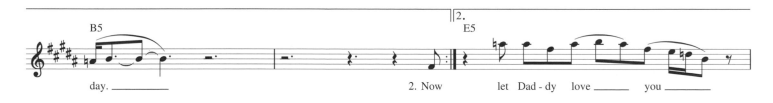

day. _____ 2. Now let Dad - dy love _____ you _____

Five Long Years

Words and Music by Eddie Boyd

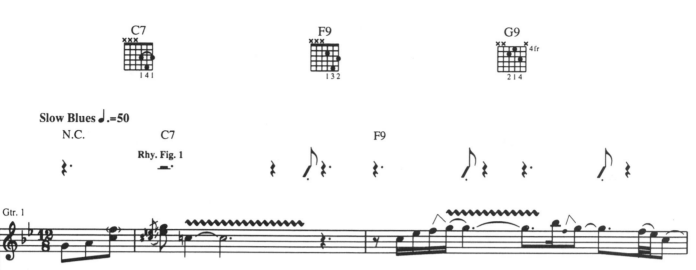

Slow Blues ♩.=50

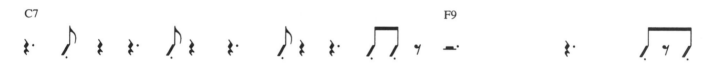

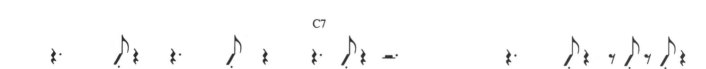

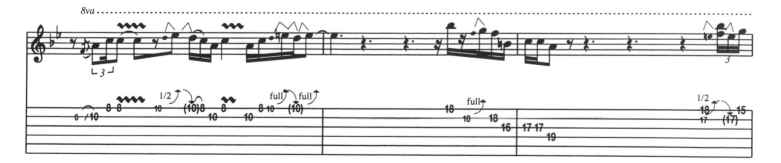

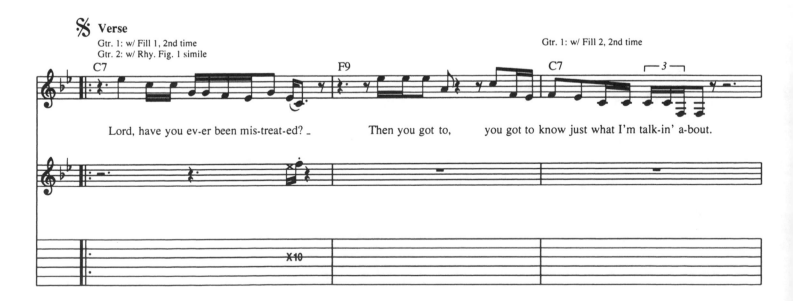

Lord, have you ev-er been mis-treat-ed? _ Then you got to, you got to know just what I'm talk-in' a-bout.

Yes, have you ev-er been mis-treat-ed? _____   Then you got to,   a you

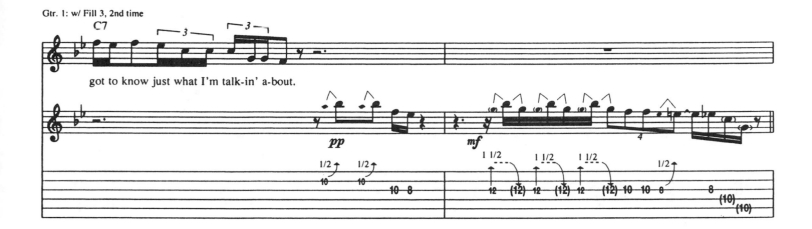

Gtr. 1: w/ Fill 3, 2nd time

got to know just what I'm talk-in' a-bout.

Fill 1
Gtr. 1

Fill 2
Gtr. 1

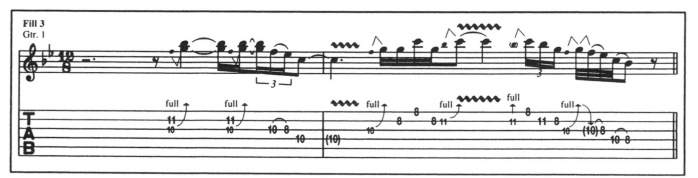

Fill 3
Gtr. 1

I should have know long time a-go.

The next wom-an I mar-ry, she got to have two jobs and she got to go out and

work long and bring some dough.

Lord, said I been mis-treat-ed,

and you got to, you got to know just what I'm talk-in' a-bout.

Fill 8
Gtr. 1

Fill 11
Gtr. 2

Fill 10
Gtr. 1

Gtr. 1: w/ Fill 12, on D.S.S.

To Coda 2

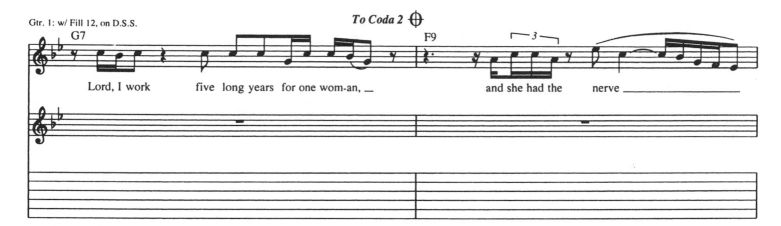

Lord, I work five long years for one wom-an, and she had the nerve

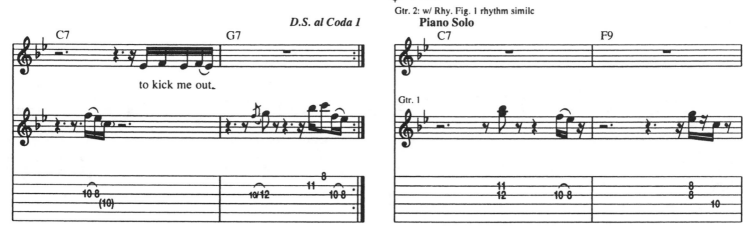

Coda

Gtr. 2: w/ Rhy. Fig. 1 rhythm simile
Piano Solo

D.S. al Coda 1

to kick me out.

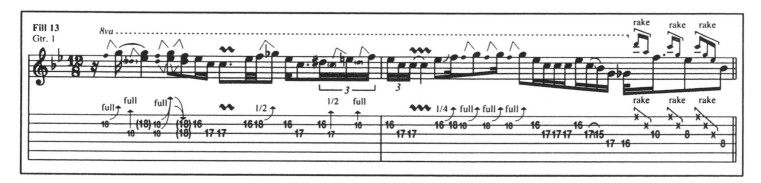

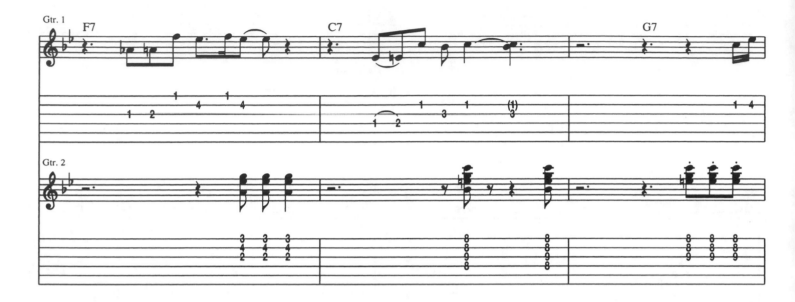

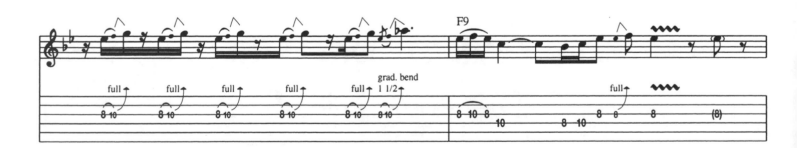

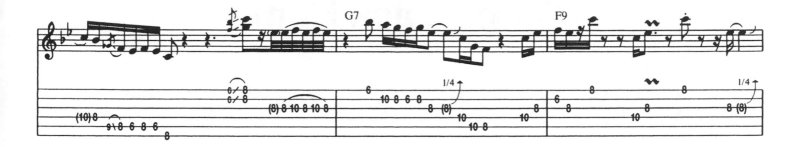

D.S.S. al Coda 2

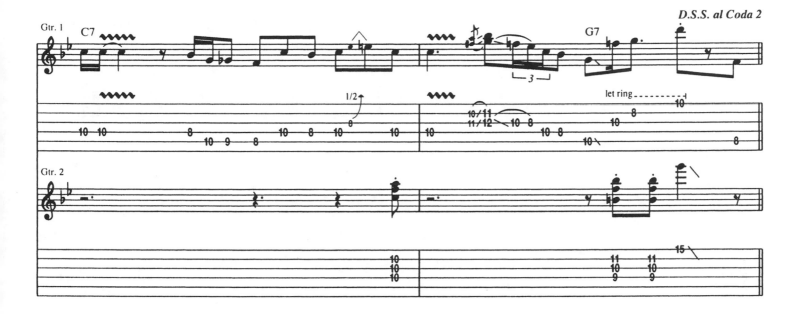

✛ *Coda 2*

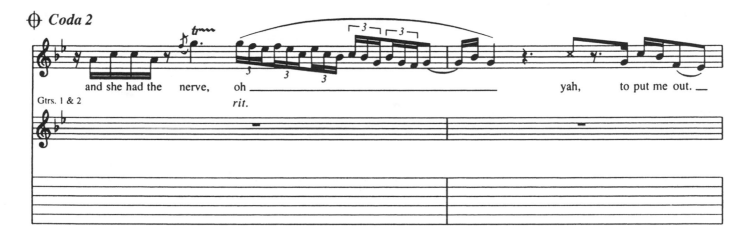

and she had the   nerve,   oh _____   yah,   to put me out. __

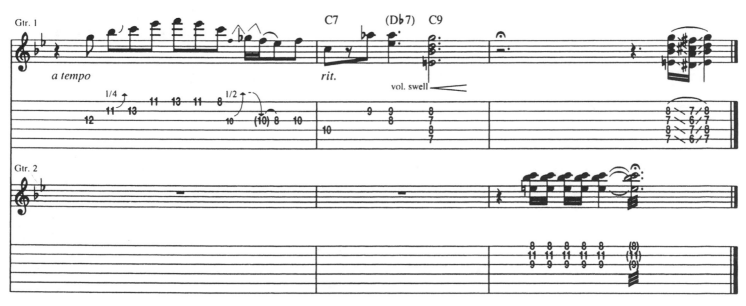

Going Back Home

By Son Seals

Intro
Slow Blues ♩. = 57

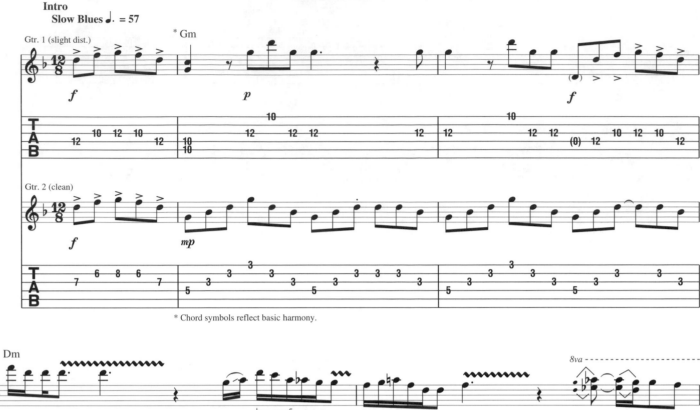

* Chord symbols reflect basic harmony.

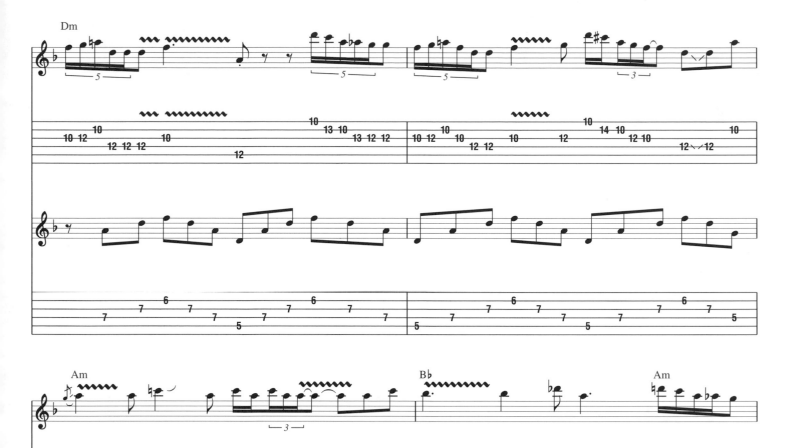

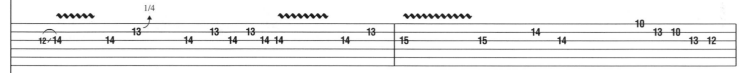

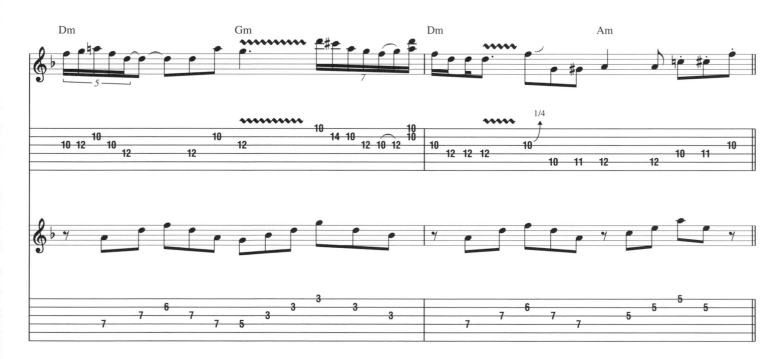

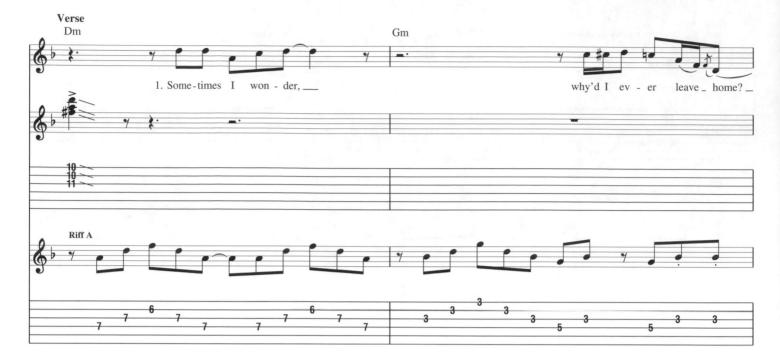

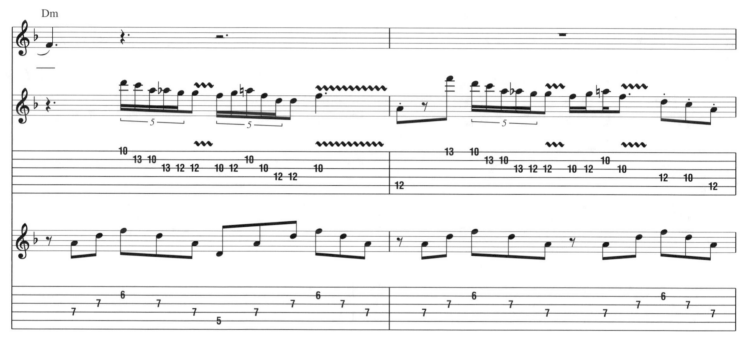

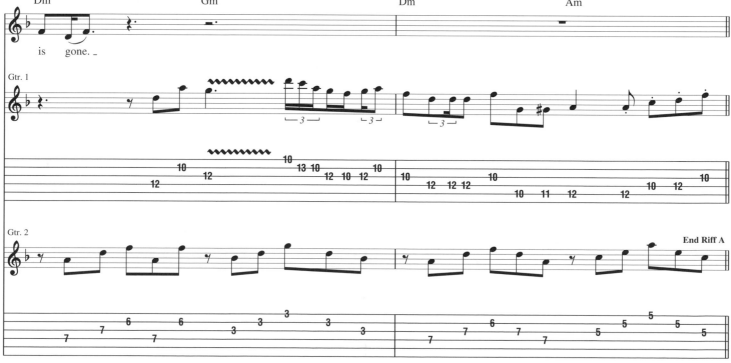

Verse

Gtr. 2: w/ Riff A

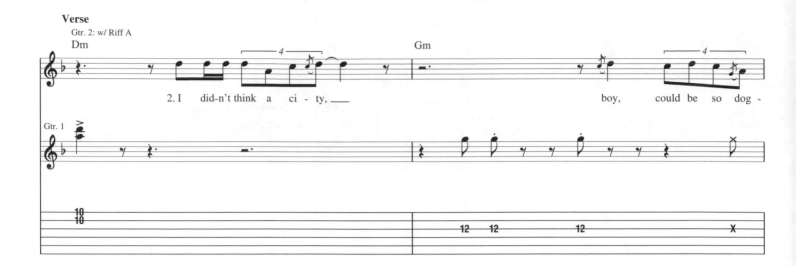

2. I did-n't think a ci - ty, _____ boy, could be so dog -

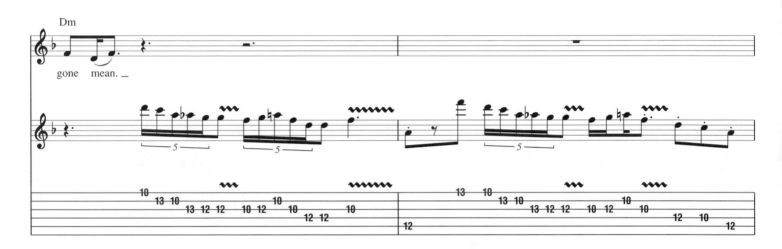

gone mean. _

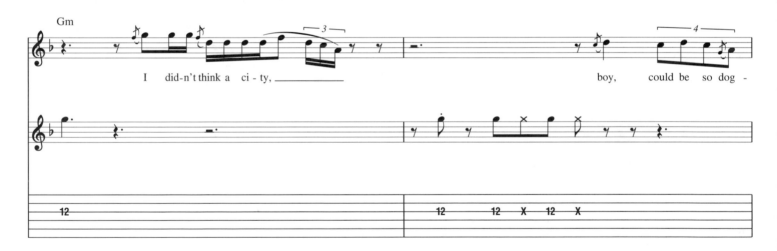

I did-n't think a ci - ty, _____ boy, could be so dog -

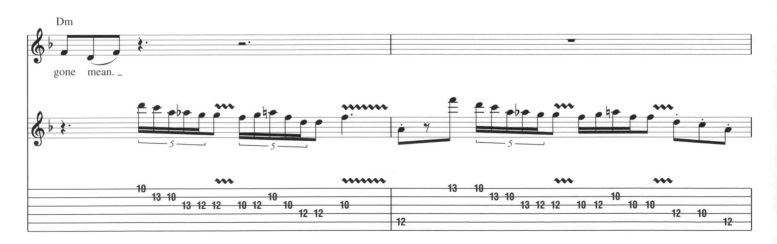

gone mean. _

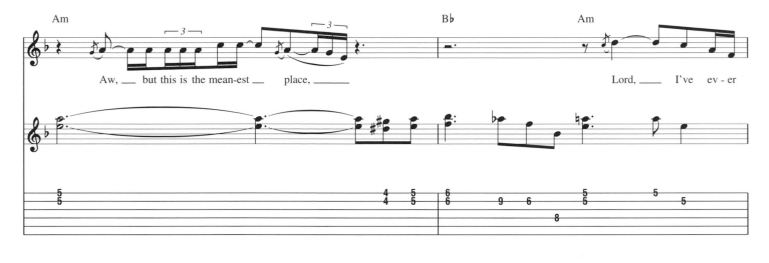

Aw, ___ but this is the mean-est ___ place, ___ Lord, ___ I've ev - er

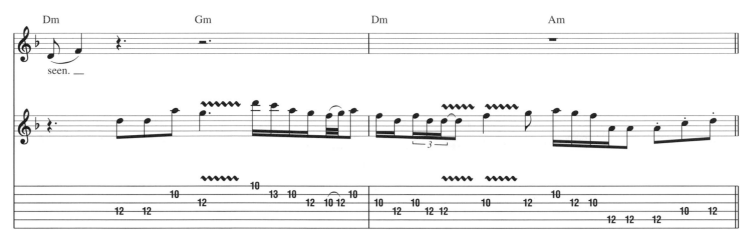

seen. ___

Verse

Gtr. 2: w/ Riff A

3. I used to have a job ___ do- in' spot la - bor ev - 'ry

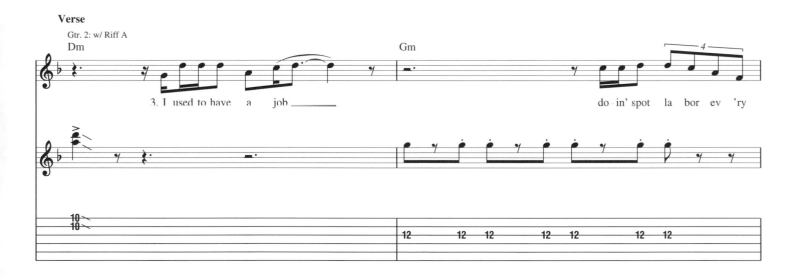

day. ___

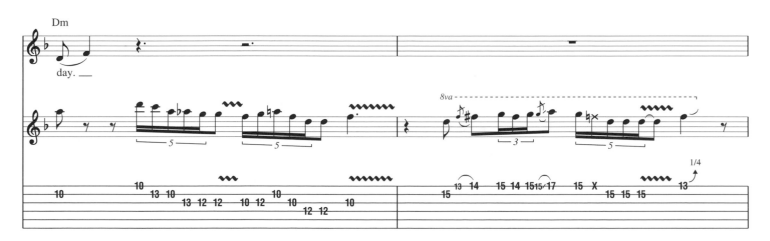

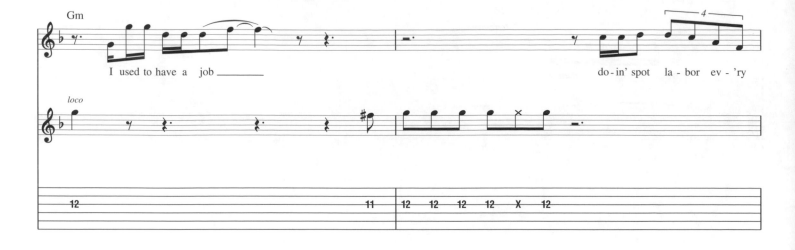

Gm

I used to have a job _____ do-in' spot la - bor ev - 'ry

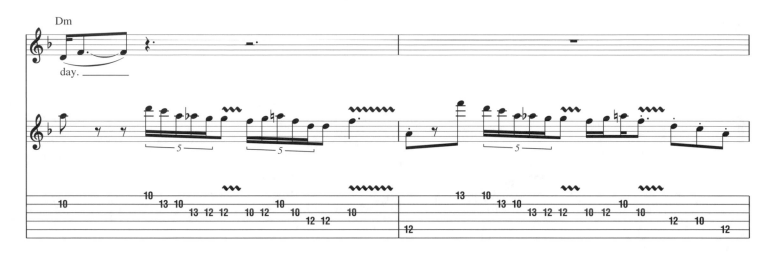

Dm

day. _____

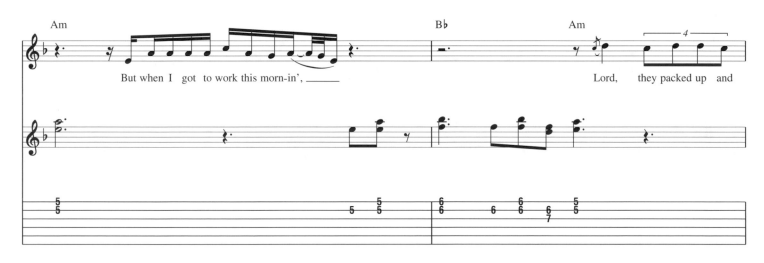

Am   B♭   Am

But when I got to work this morn-in', _____ Lord,   they packed up   and

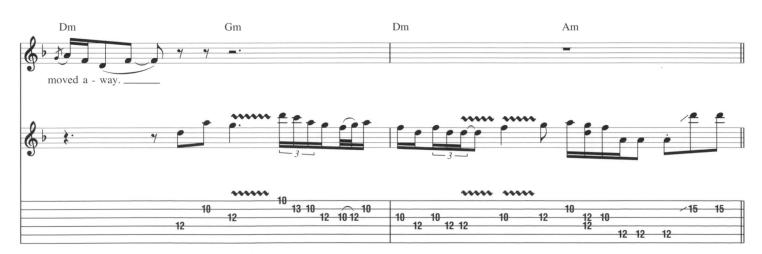

Dm   Gm   Dm   Am

moved a - way. _____

Guitar Solo

Gtr. 2: w/ Riff A

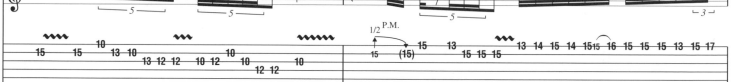

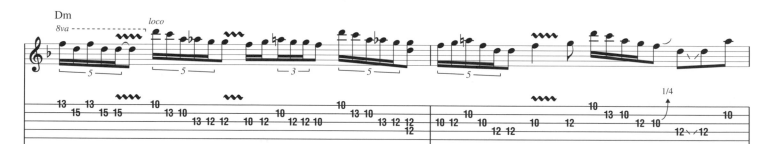

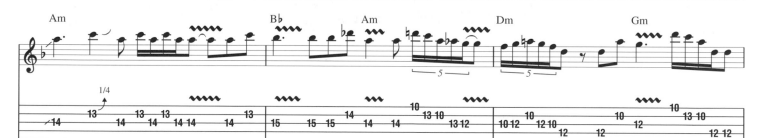

Verse

Gtr. 2: w/ Riff A

4. I called my boss. ___ I wan-na know, can I ___

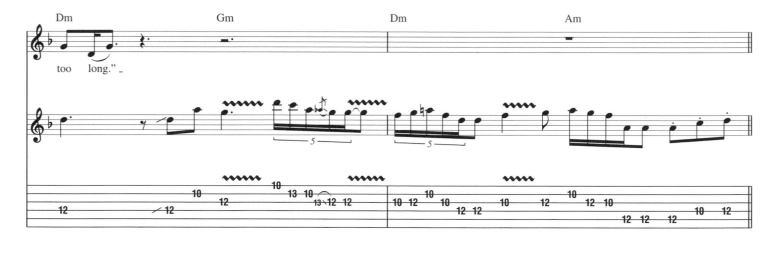

Verse
Gtr. 2: w/ Riff A

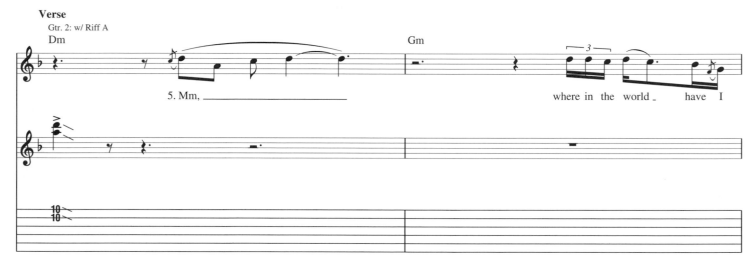

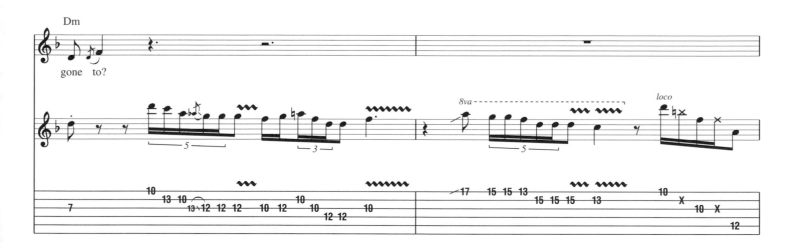

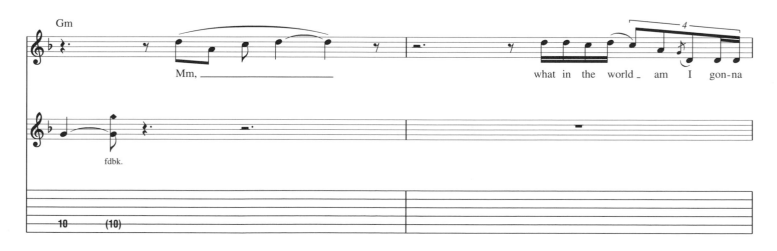

I guess it's just all wrapped up in a nut-shell now. Oh, __ it looked like old __ poor Son's gon-na be.

Guitar Solo

Gtr. 1: w/ Riff A (1st 10 meas.)

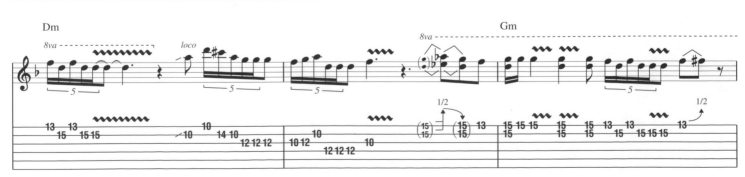

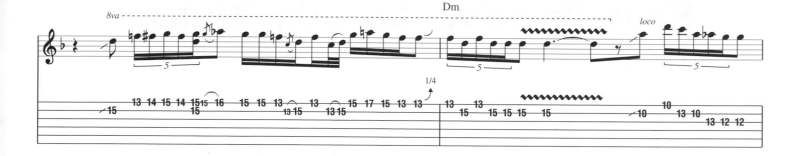

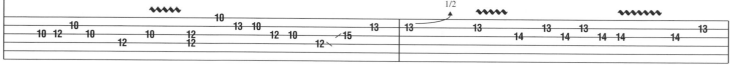

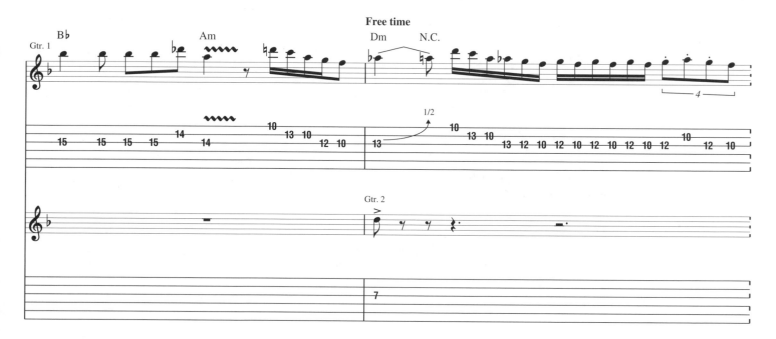

Have You Ever Loved a Woman

Words and Music by Billy Myles

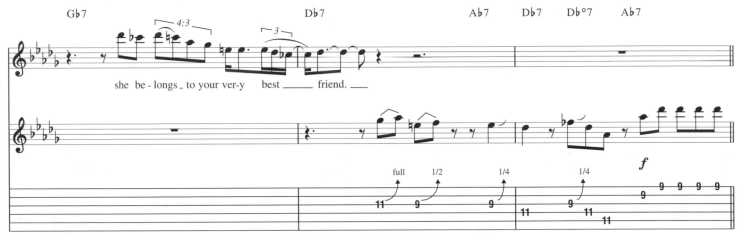

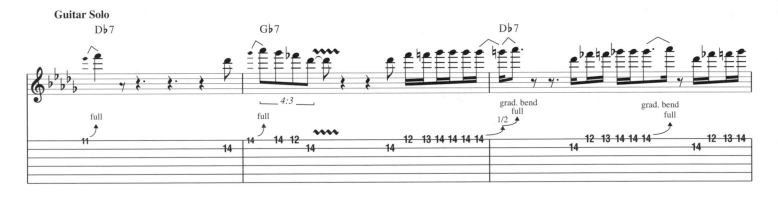

Guitar Solo

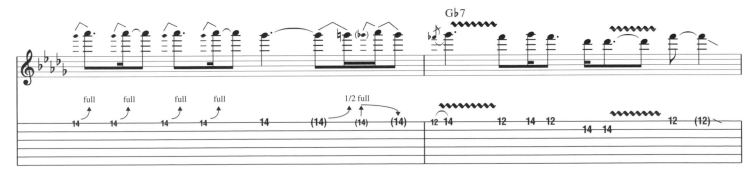

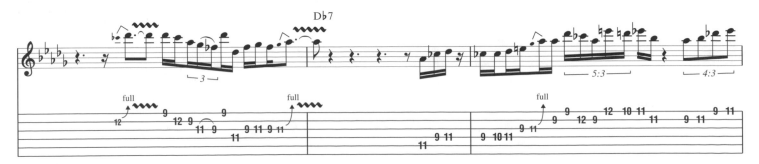

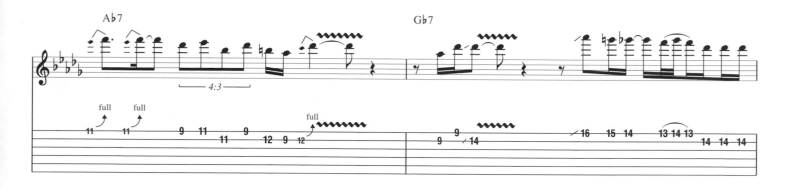

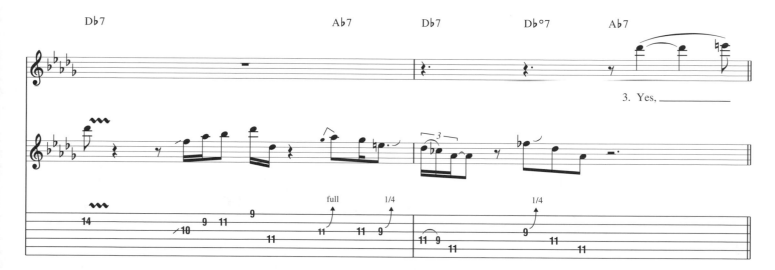

3. Yes, _____

Verse

have you ev - er loved _ a wom - an, _ one that _ you know _ you can't leave _ a - lone?

Yeah, _____

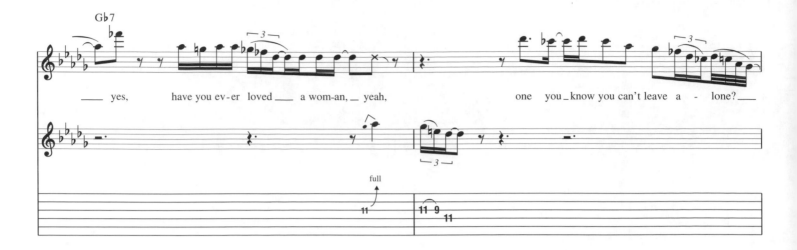

_____ yes, have you ev-er loved _____ a wom-an, _____ yeah, one you_ know you can't leave a - lone?_____

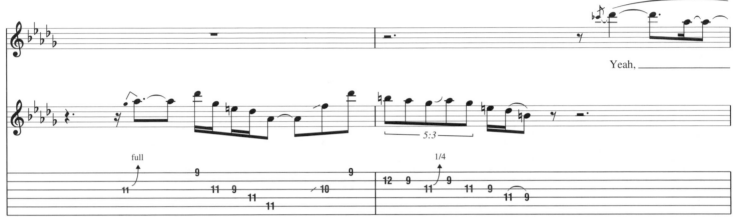

Yeah, _____

_____ yes, 'cause there's some-thing deep in - side of you_____ won't let you wreck your best friend's_ home._

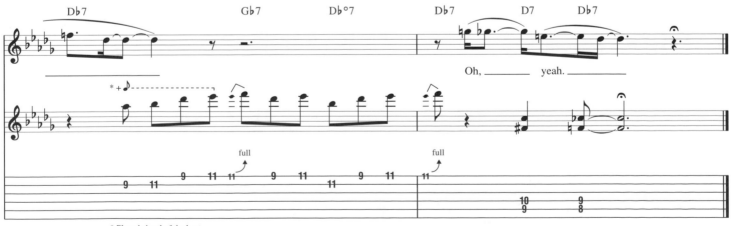

Oh, _____ yeah. _____

* Played ahead of the beat.

The Healer

By John Lee Hooker, Roy Rogers, Carlos Santana and Chester Thompson

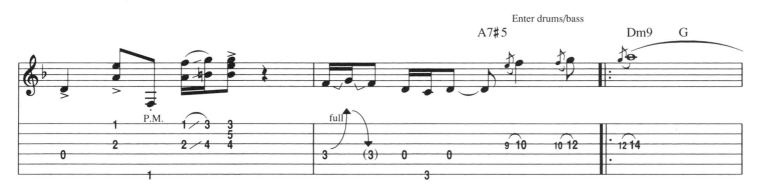

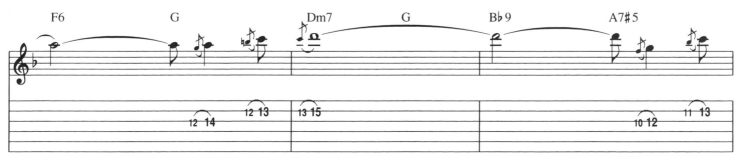

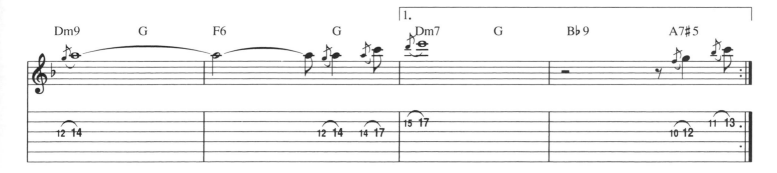

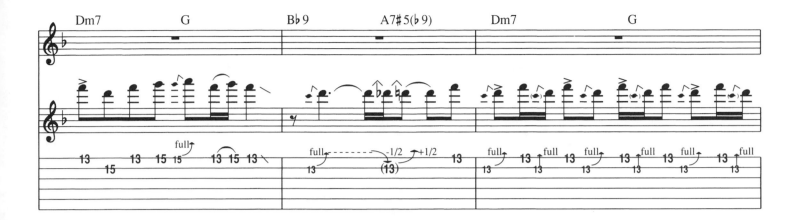

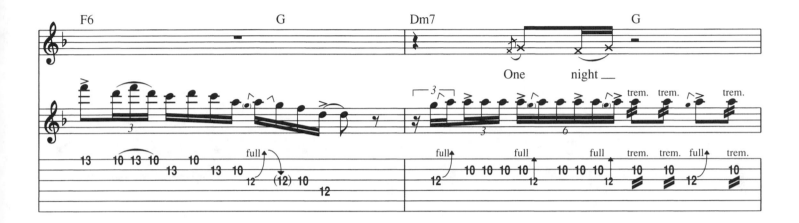

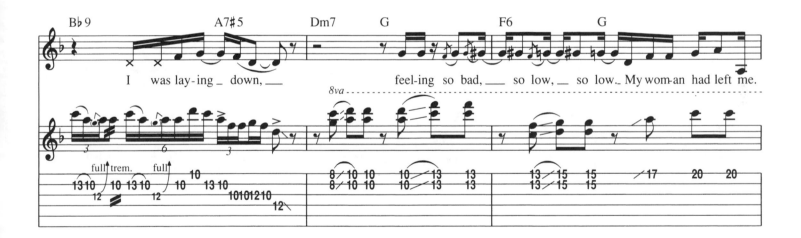

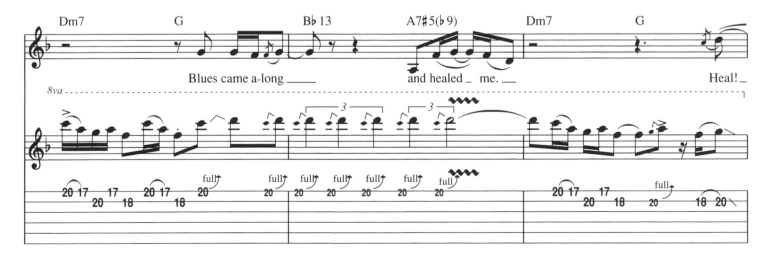

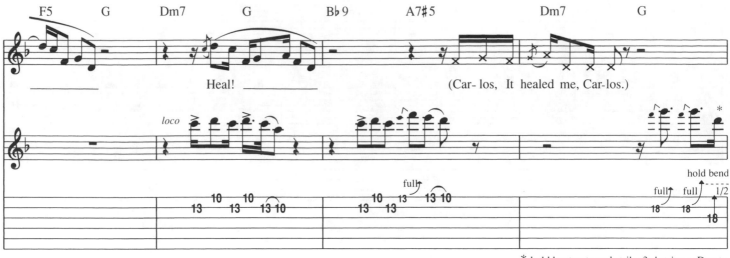

* hold bent note and strike 3rd string = D note

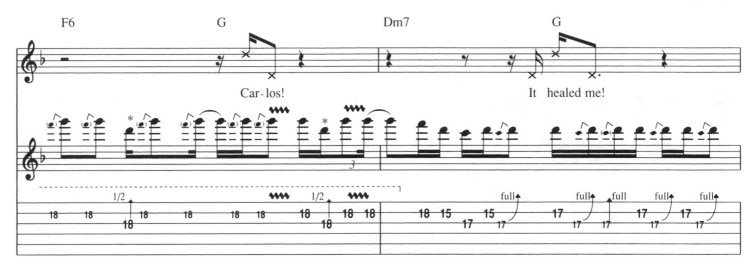

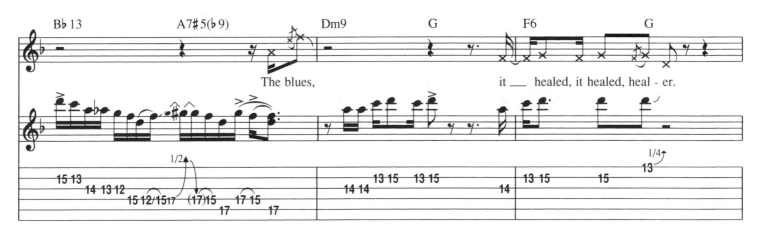

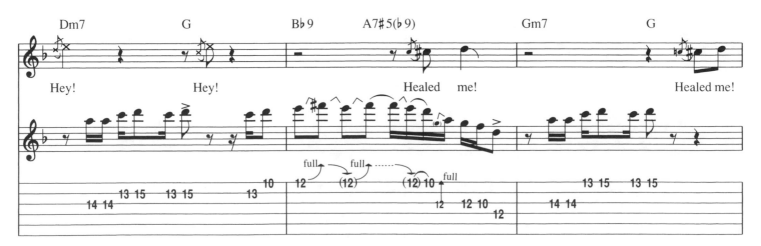

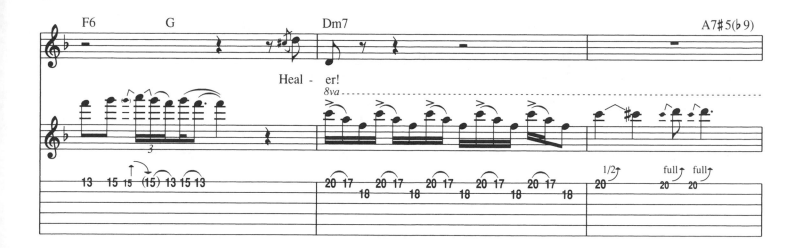

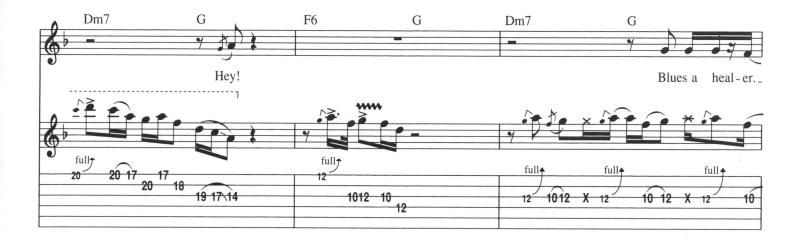

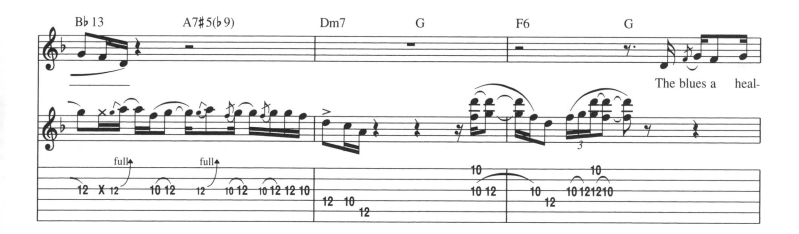

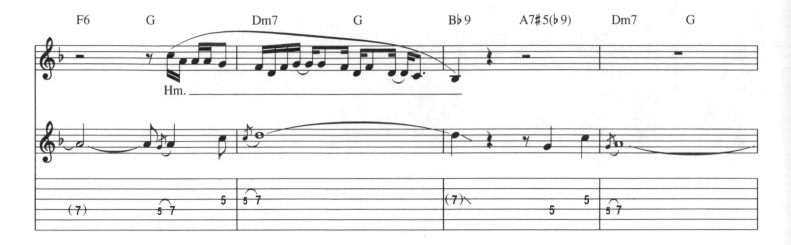

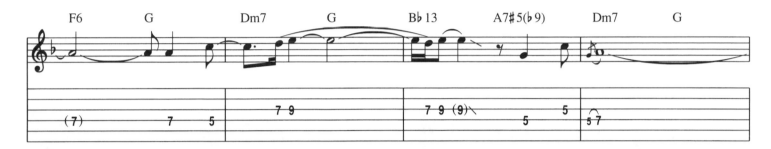

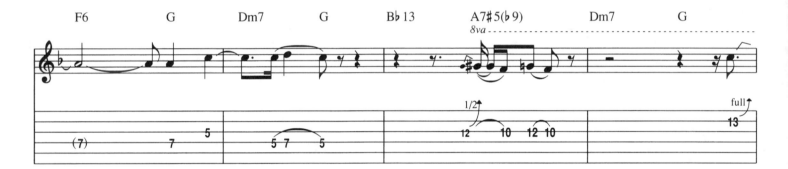

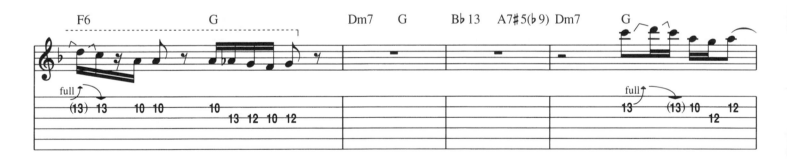

all _ o-ver the world,_ all _ o — ver the world. _____ Lord, __ Lord, _ Lord, _ Lord, Lord. _____

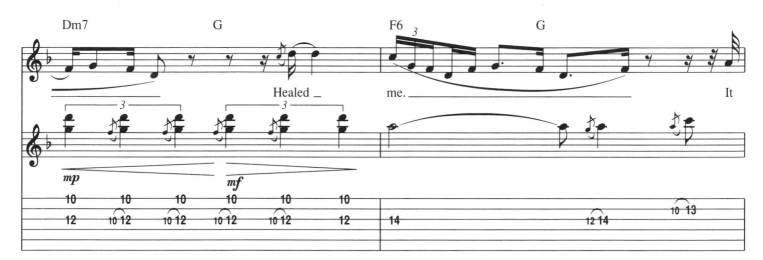

Healed _ me. _____ It

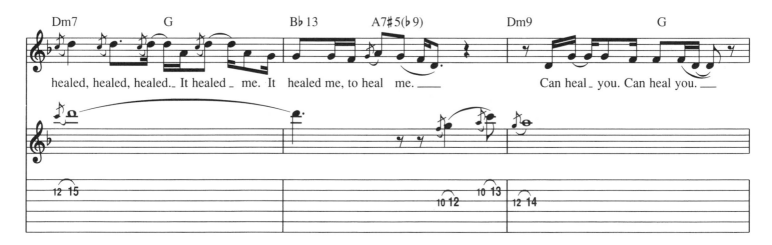

healed, healed, healed._ It healed _ me. It _ healed me, to heal _ me. ____ Can heal _ you. Can heal you. ____

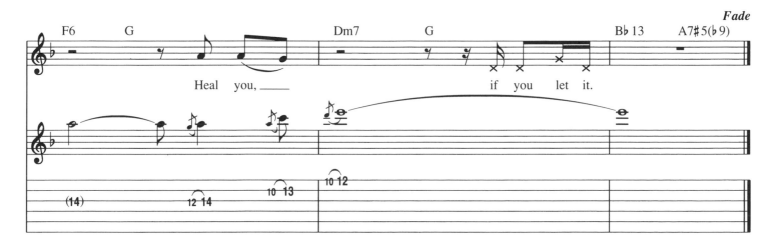

Heal _ you, _____ if _ you _ let _ it.

I Ain't Got You

By Calvin Carter

*Chord symbols reflect overall harmony.

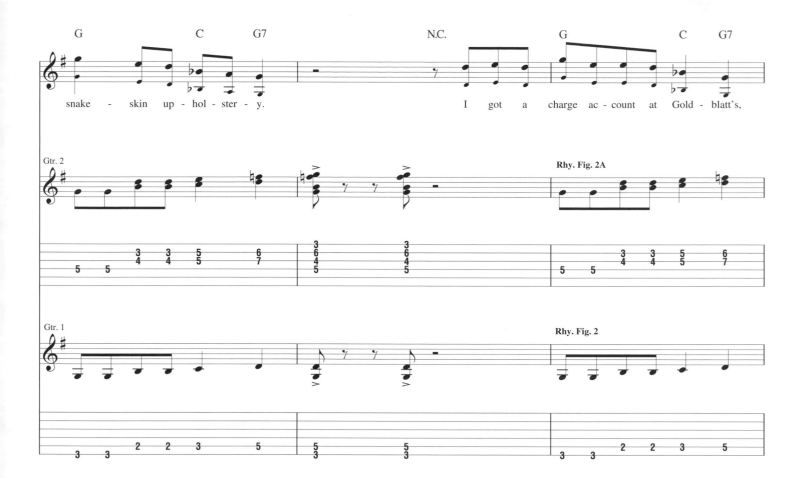

snake - skin up - hol - ster - y. I got a charge ac - count at Gold - blatt's,

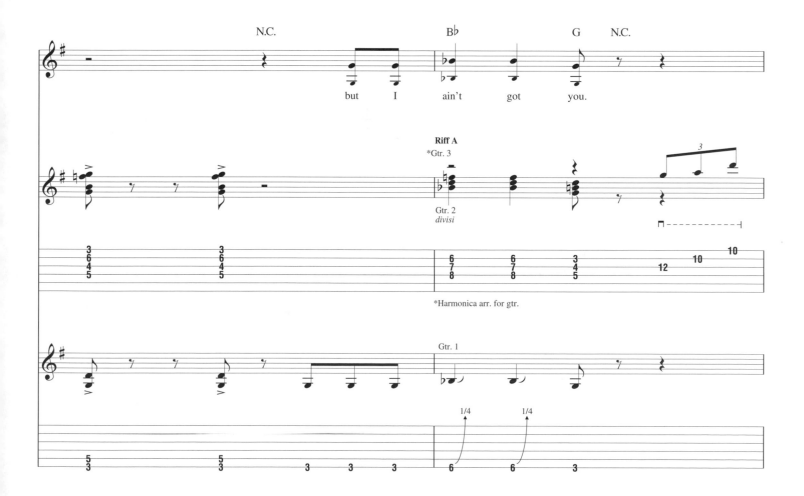

but I ain't got you.

*Harmonica arr. for gtr.

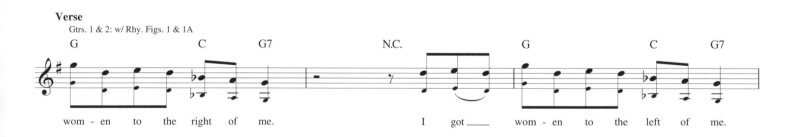

*Composite arrangement.

I got a

(Gtr. 2 cont. in slashes)

ain't   got   you.   No,   I   ain't   got   you.

I Can't Quit You Baby

Written by Willie Dixon

you messed up my hap-py home ba-by.   You made ___ me mis-treat ___ my

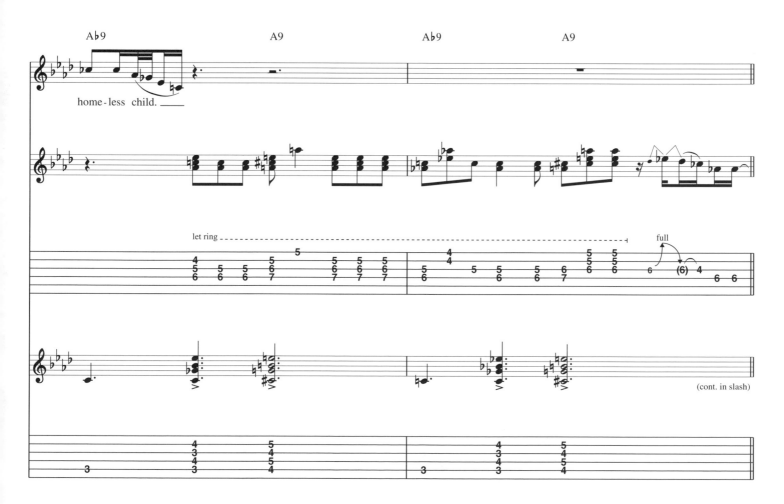

home-less child. ___

(cont. in slash)

Verse

2. Yes, you know I love you, babe.

My love for you I could never hide.

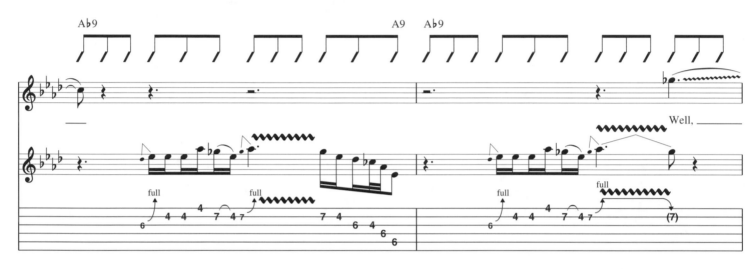

Well,

you know I love you, babe.

My love for you I could never hide.

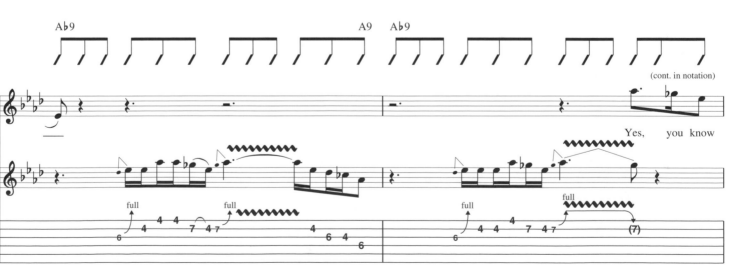

(cont. in notation)

Yes, you know

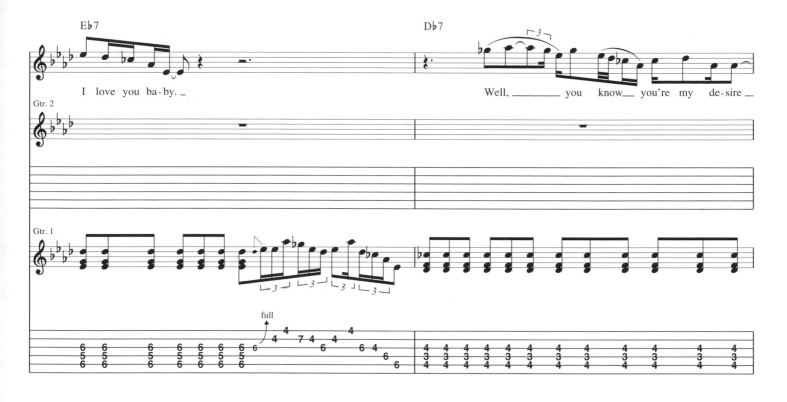

I love you ba-by. ___

Well, _____ you know___ you're my de-sire ___

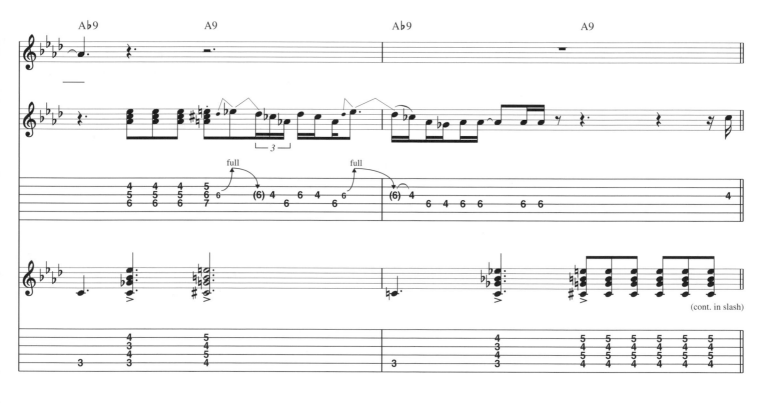

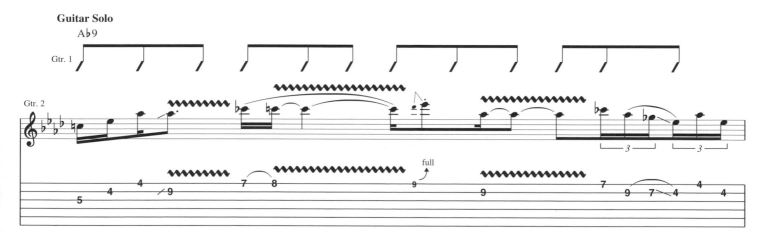

Guitar Solo

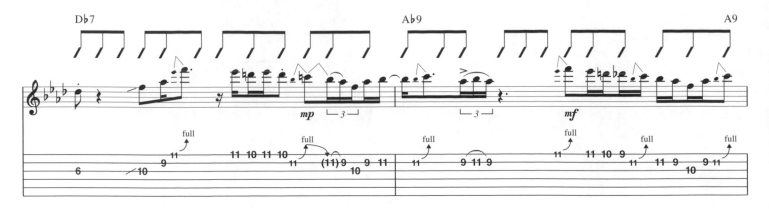

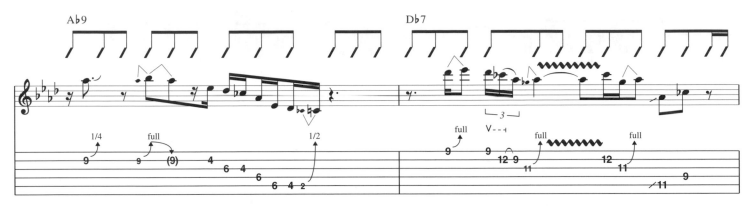

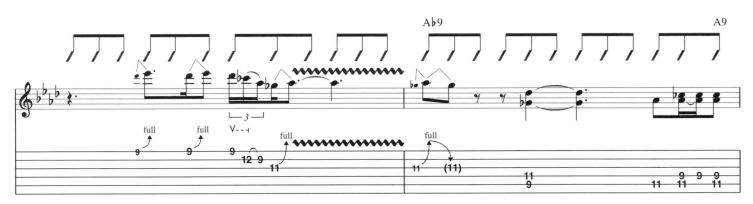

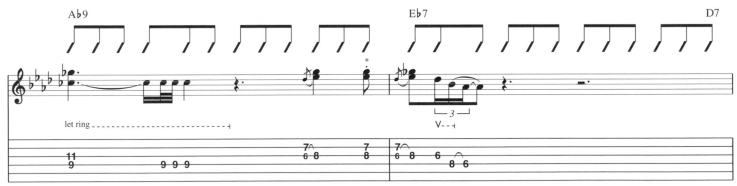

* Only lower note is played staccato.

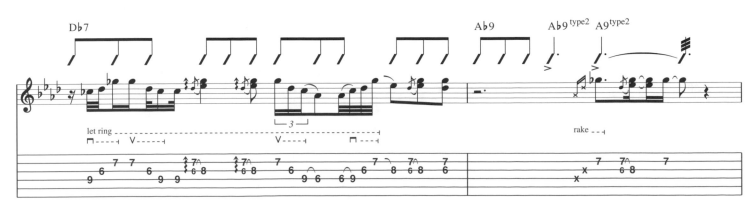

94

Yes, when you hear me hol - ler, ba - by,

well, _____ you know_____ you're my de - sire. _____

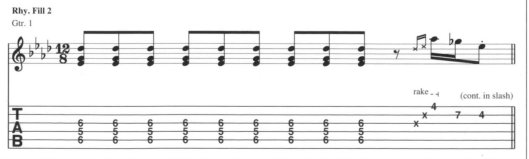

I Got a Break Baby

Words and Music by Aaron "T-Bone" Walker

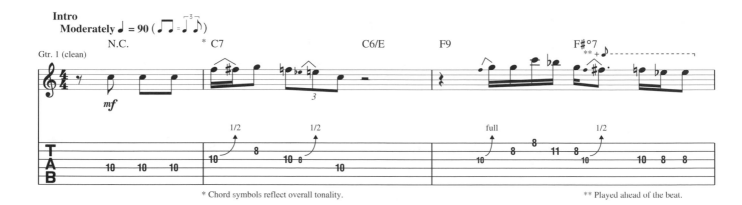

* Chord symbols reflect overall tonality. ** Played ahead of the beat.

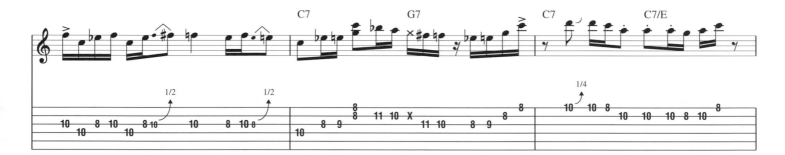

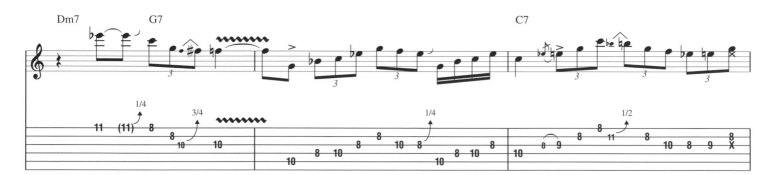

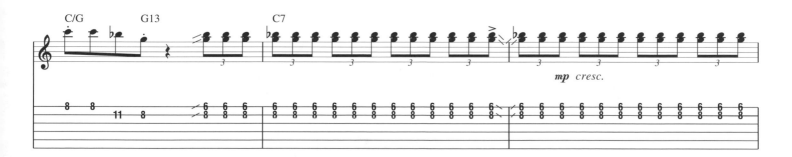

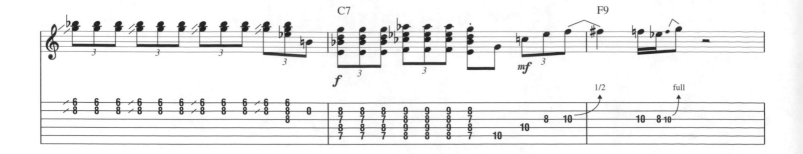

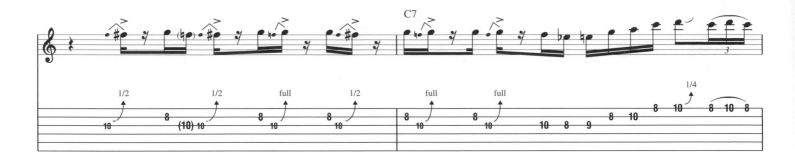

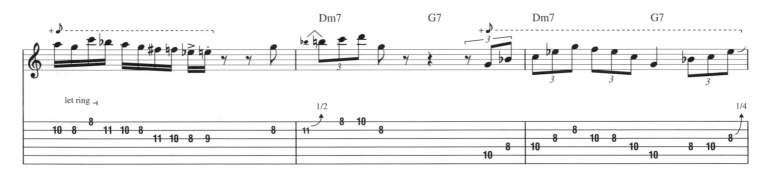

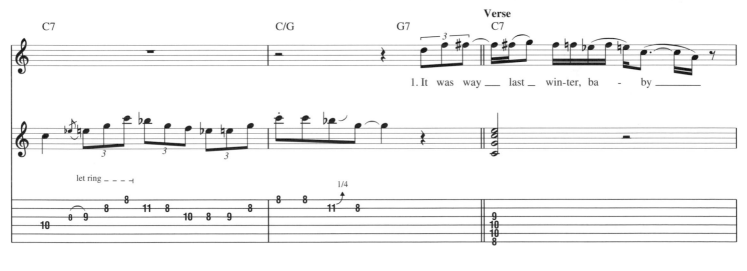

1. It was way ___ last ___ win-ter, ba - by ___

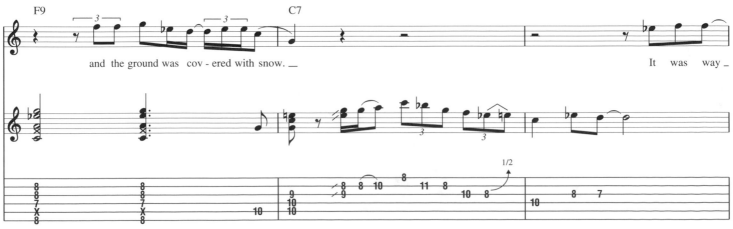

and the ground was cov-ered with snow. ___

It was way ___

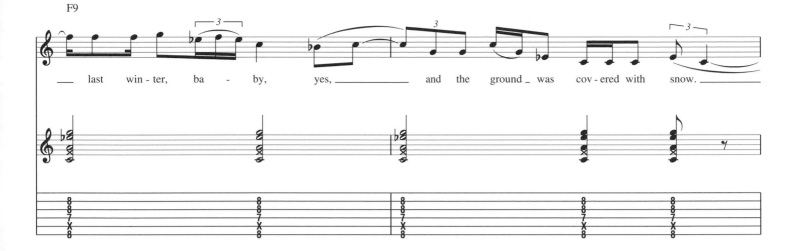

last win-ter, ba — by, yes, _____ and the ground _ was cov-ered with snow. _____

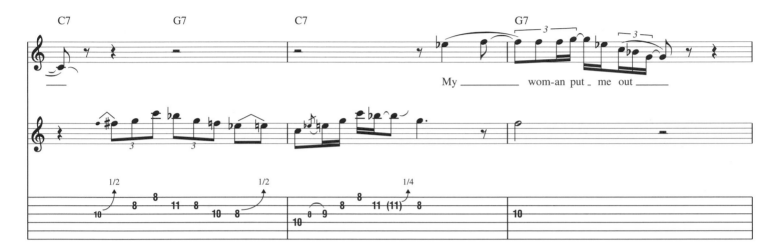

My _____ wom-an put _ me out _____

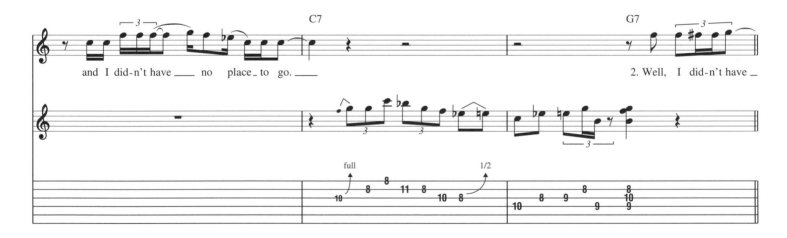

and I did-n't have _____ no place _ to go. _____ 2. Well, I did-n't have _

Verse

_____ no _ mon-ey, dar - lin' _____ and my shoes _ had worn thin. _____

I _____ grabbed _ my hat, ba - by, and I did not e - ven run. ___

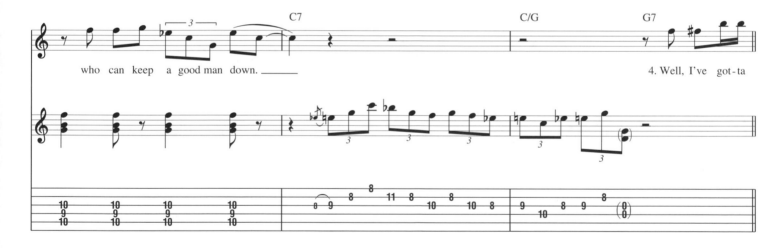

___ I ain't know one wom-an ___

who can keep a good man down. _____ 4. Well, I've got-ta

Verse

break, ba - by, _____ and things are com-in' my way. ___

I'll Play the Blues for You

Words and Music by Jerry Beach

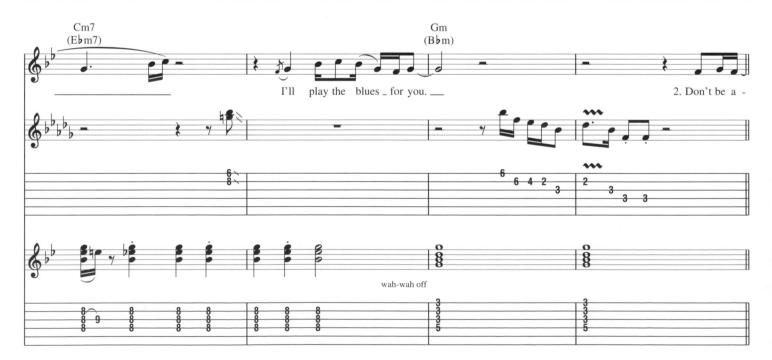

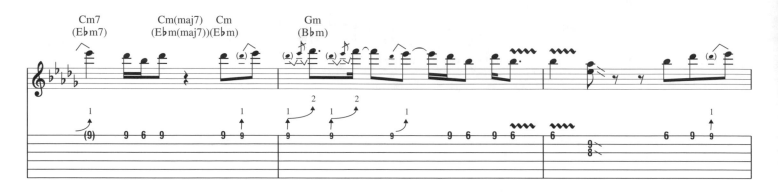

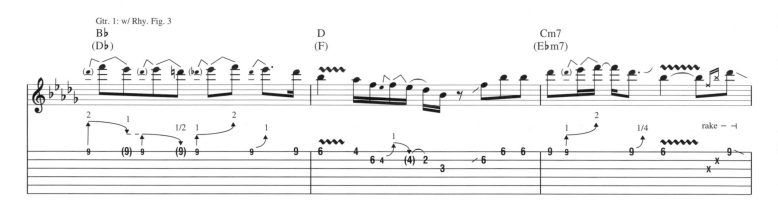

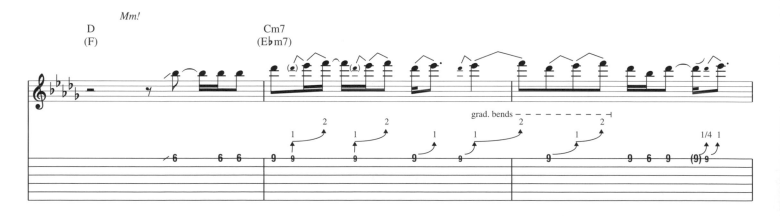

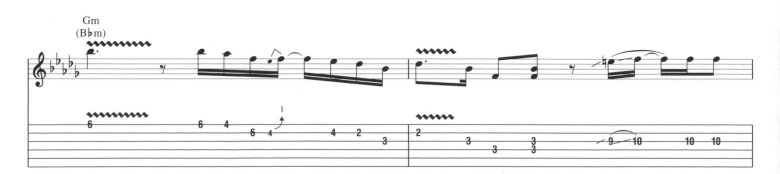

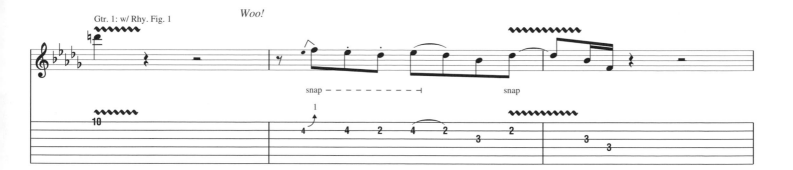

Woo!

Uh huh, yeah.

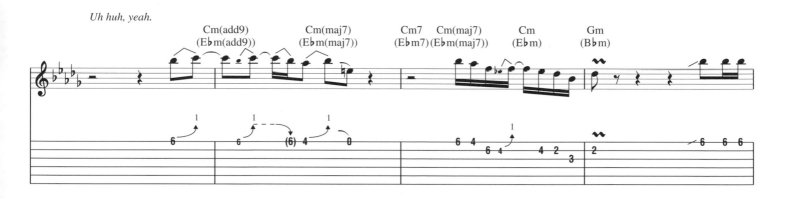

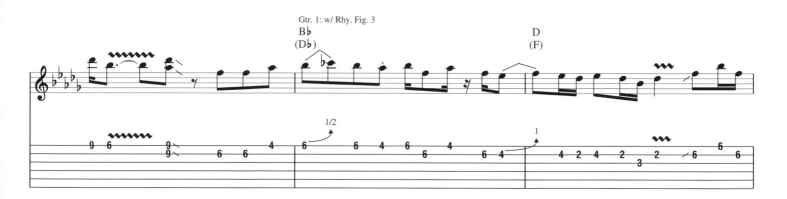

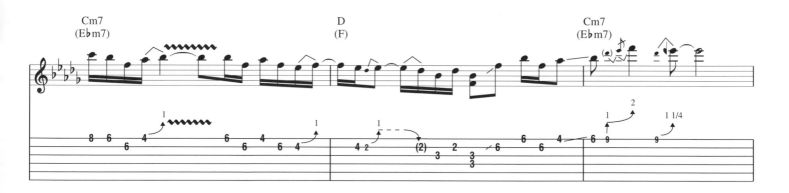

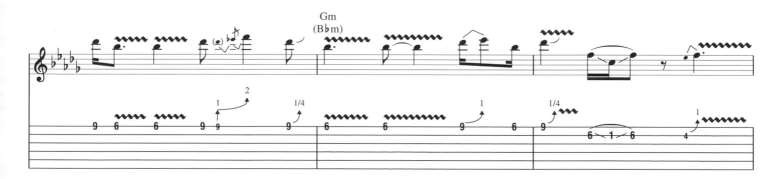

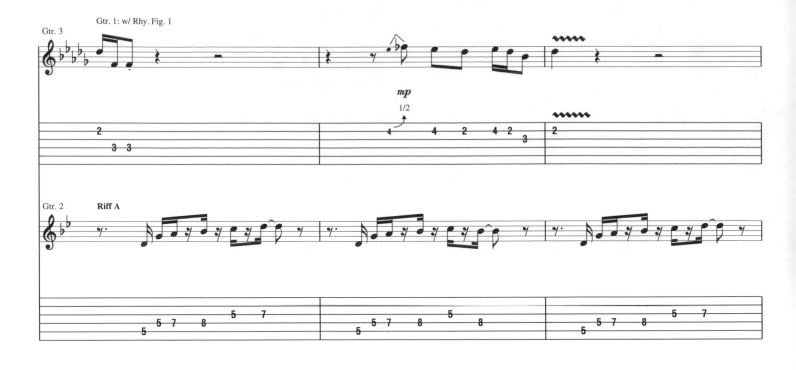

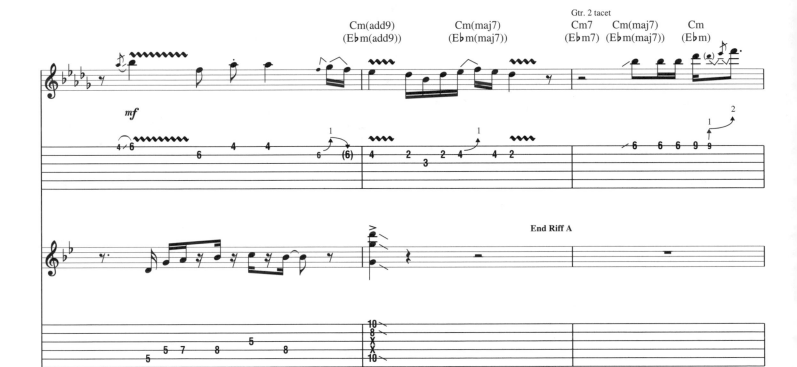

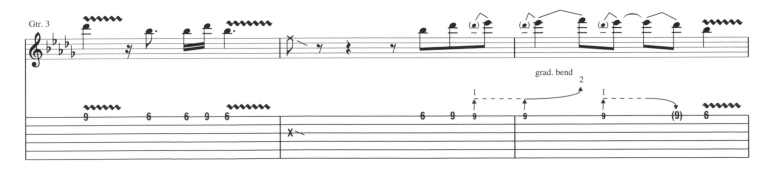

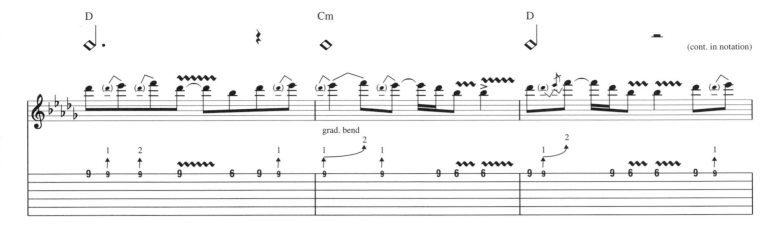

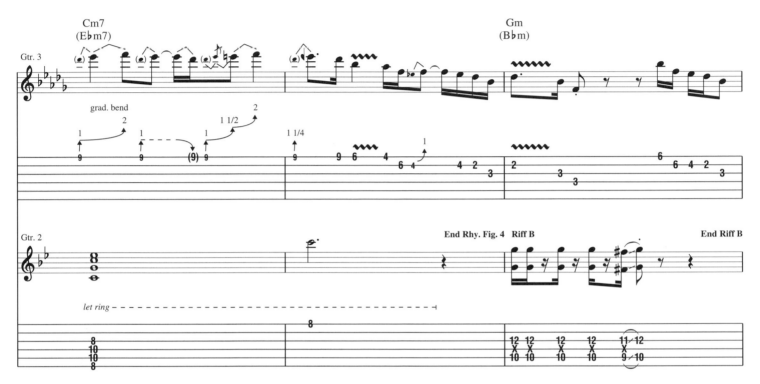

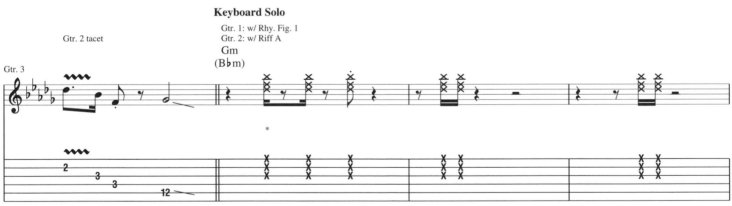

Keyboard Solo

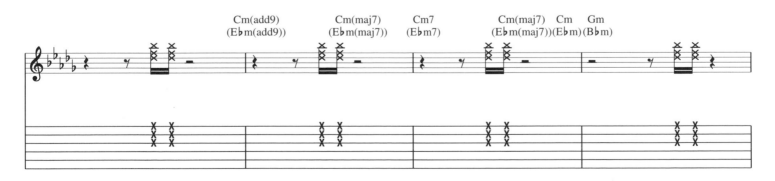

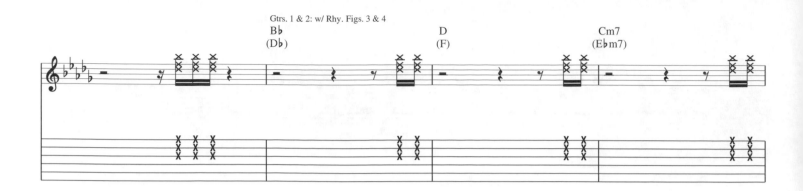

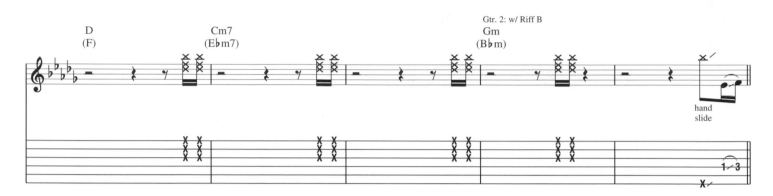

Guitar Solo

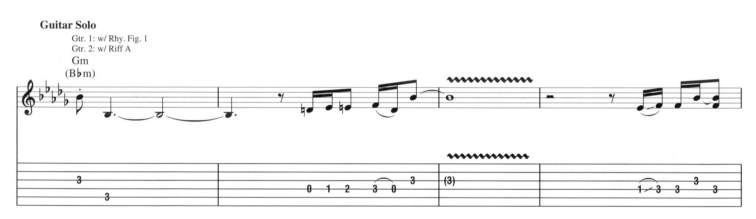

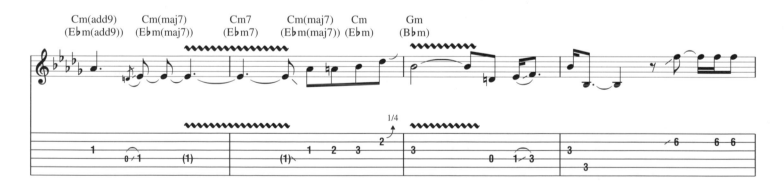

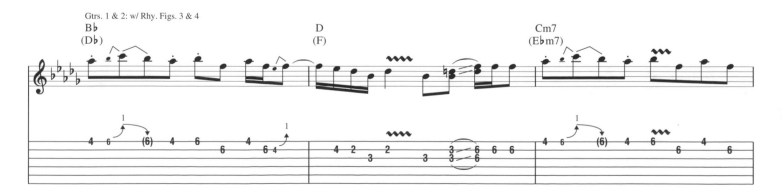

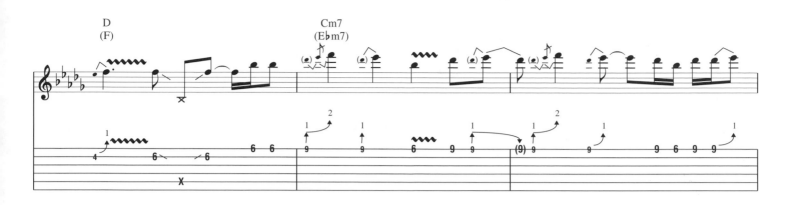

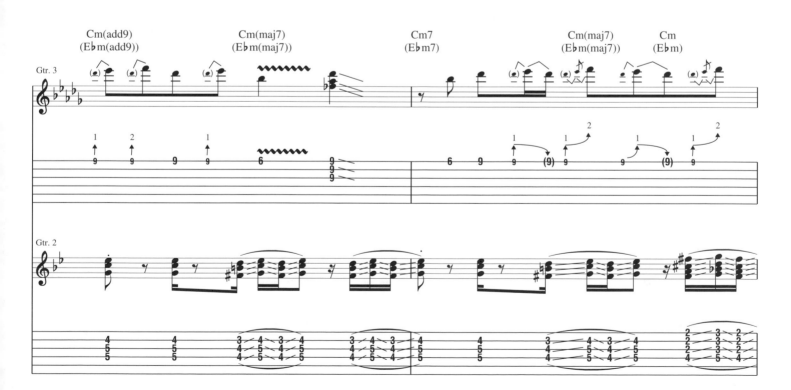

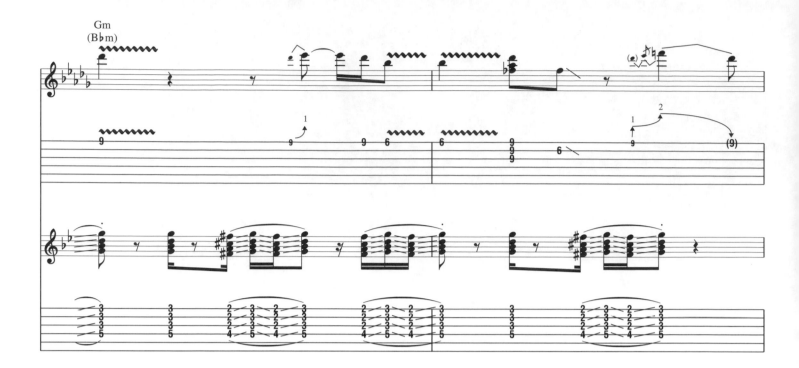

Gtrs. 1 & 2: w/ Rhy. Figs. 3 & 4

Gtr. 3

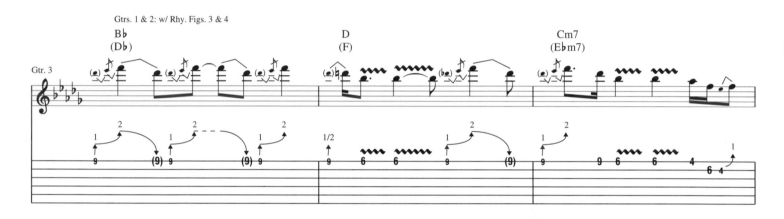

No!

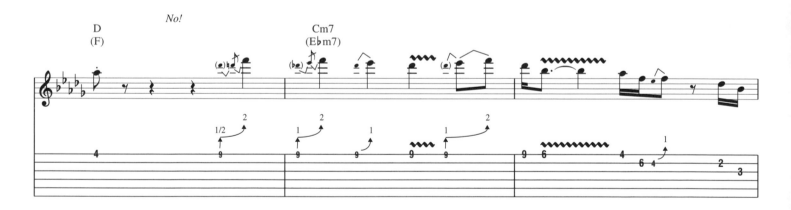

Begin fade   ***Fade out***

Gtr. 2: w/ Riff B (2 times)

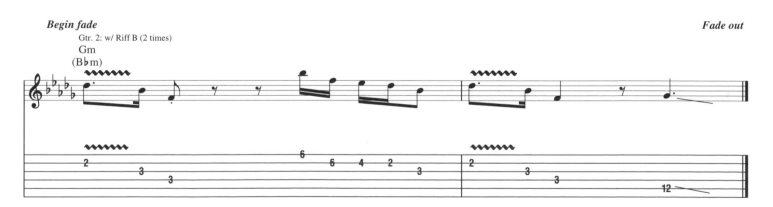

I'm Your Hoochie Coochie Man

Written by Willie Dixon

*Symbols in parenthesis represent chord names respective to capoed guitar. Symbols above reflect actual sounding chord.

Love in Vain Blues

Words and Music by Robert Johnson

and I could not help but cry. ___ All my love's in vain. ___ 3. When the

Verse

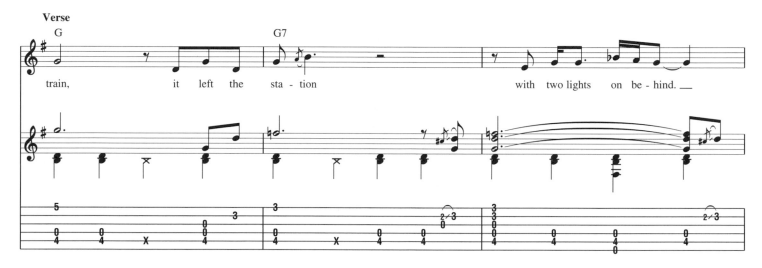

train, it left the sta - tion with two lights on be - hind. ___

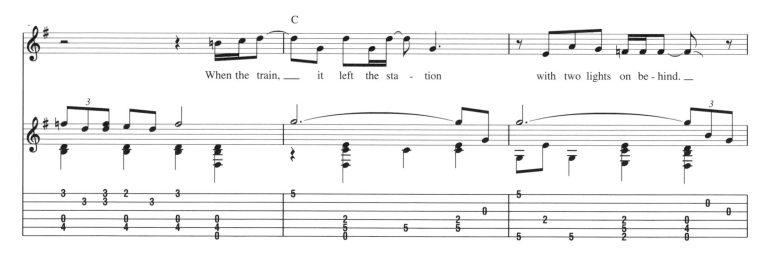

When the train, ___ it left the sta - tion with two lights on be - hind. ___

Well, the blue light was my blues

* Sung and played as even eighth notes.

119

Mannish Boy

Words and Music by McKinley Morganfield (Muddy Waters), Melvin London and Ellas McDaniel

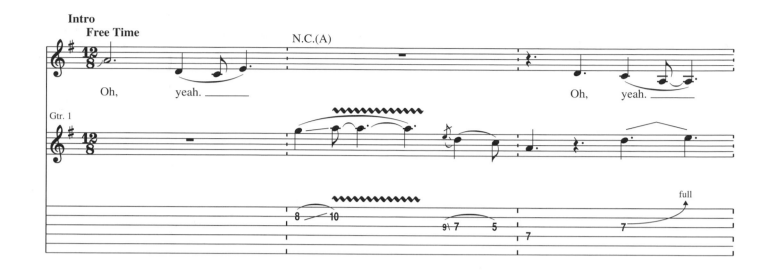

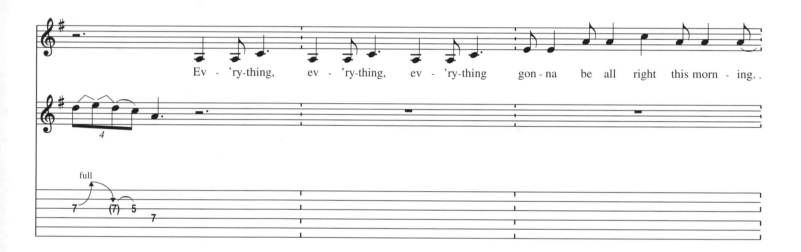

Moanin' At Midnight

Words and Music by Chester Burnett

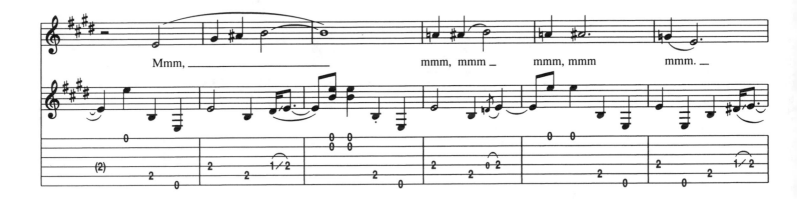

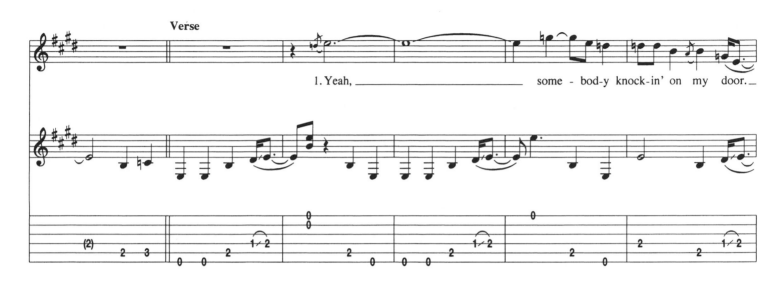

Verse

1. Yeah, _____ some - bod-y knock-in' on my door. _

Well, _____

Interlude

some - bod-y knock-in' on my door. _

2. Well, I'm __ so __ wor - ried, __ don't know __

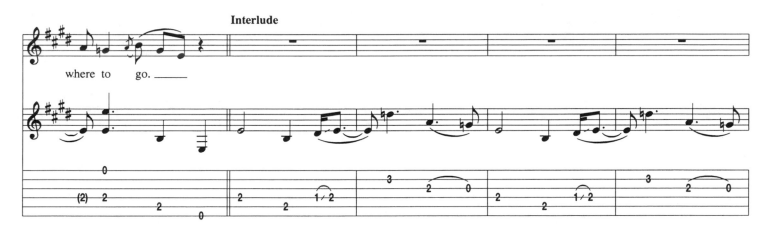

where to go. ___

3. Well, ___ some - bod - y call - in' me, call - in' me on __ my tel - e - phone. __

Well,   some - bod - y   call - in'   o - ver   my   tel - e - phone.

Interlude

Verse

4. Well, _____ keep   on ___ call - in',

tell 'em _ I'm not at _____ home. _

Hmm   doo   doo _____   doo   doo

doo   doo   doo   doo.   Mmm

hmm   doo _____   doo   doo   doo   doo

hmm. ___ Whoo. _____

Well, do ___ not ___ wor - ry,

dad - dy is ___ gone to bed. ___

One Way Out

By Sonny Boy Williamson, Elmore James and Marshall Sehorn

Intro

Moderately Bright Shuffle ♩ = 150

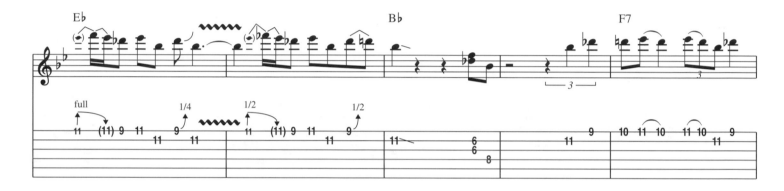

Verse

Gtr. 1: w/ Rhy. Fill 1, 2nd time
Gtr. 1: w/ Rhy. Fig. 1, 5 times, simile, 4th time

1. Raise your win-dow, ba - by, I ain't go-ing out _ that
2., 3., 4. See Additional Lyrics

Rhy. Fill 1

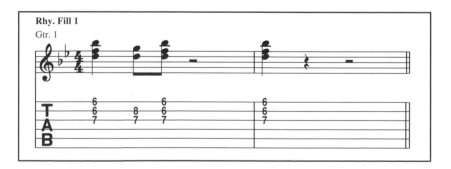

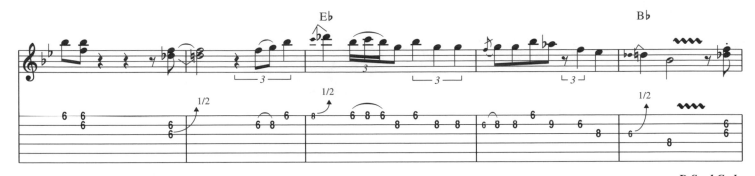

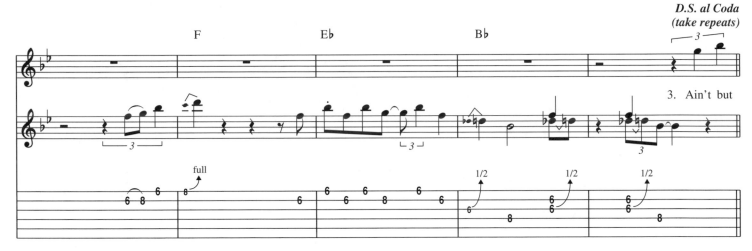

D.S. al Coda
(take repeats)

3. Ain't but

more.

Additional Lyrics

2. I said raise your window, baby, let me ease out real slow, oh yeah.
   Raise your window, baby, let me ease out real slow.
   Your neighbors can't start a-talkin' a lot of junk that they don't know, oh no.

3. Ain't but one way out, I ain't goin' out that door.
   Ain't but one way out, baby, I ain't goin' out that door.
   I want you to raise your window one time, let me out real slow.

4. I said raise, I said raise it,
   I said raise, I said raise it.
   If I get away this time, I won't be comin' back here no more.

Pride and Joy

Written by Stevie Ray Vaughan

Verse

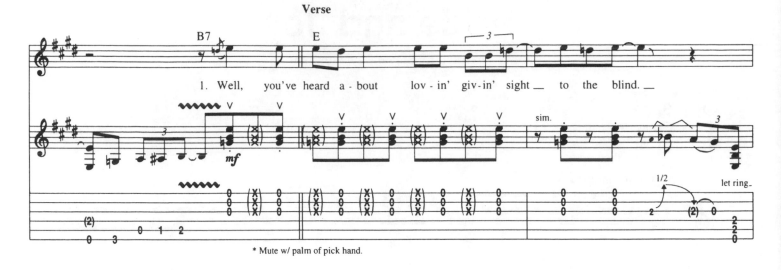

1. Well, you've heard a-bout lov-in' giv-in' sight __ to the blind. __

* Mute w/ palm of pick hand.

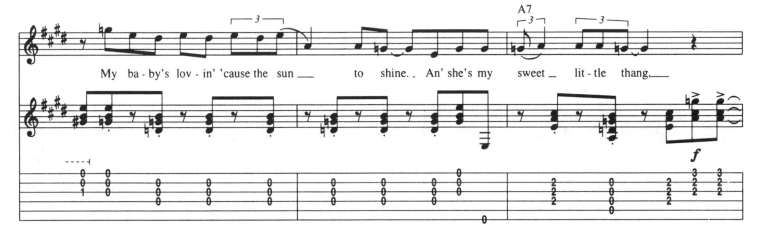

My ba-by's lov-in' 'cause the sun __ to shine.. An' she's my sweet __ lit-tle thang, __

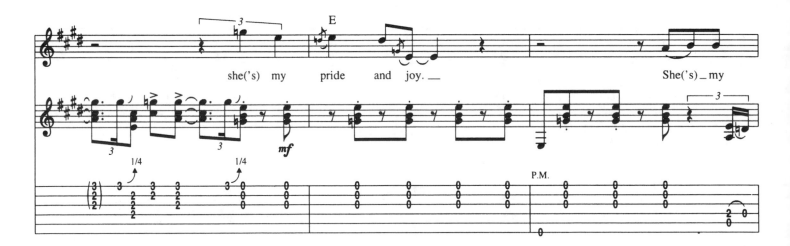

she('s) my pride and joy. __ She('s) __ my

sweet lit-tle ba-by, I'm __ her __ lit-tle lov-er boy. __

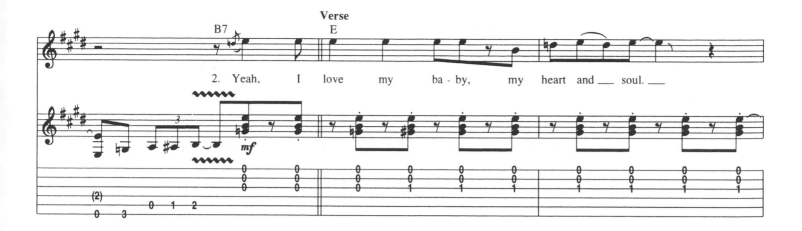

Verse

2. Yeah, I love my ba - by, my heart and __ soul. __

Love like ours __ ah, won't nev - er grow __ old. She('s) my sweet __ lit - tle thang, __

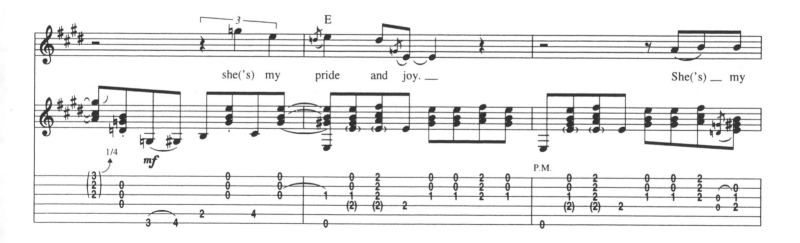

she('s) my pride and joy. __ She('s) __ my

sweet lit - tle ba - by, I'm __ her lit - tle lov - er boy. __

sweet _ lit - tle ba - by, I'm __ her __ lit - tle lov - er boy. __

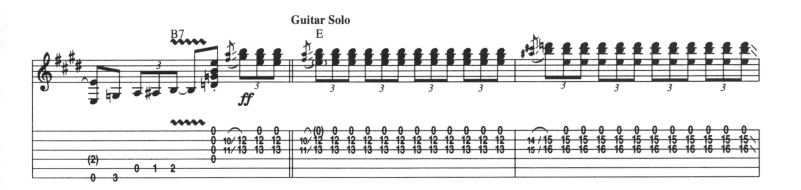

Guitar Solo

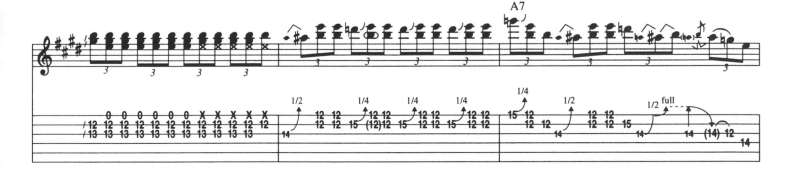

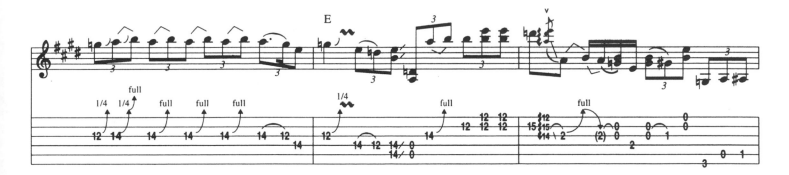

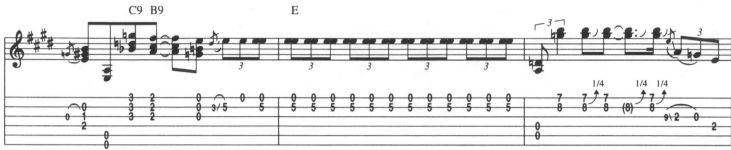

Verse

4. Well, I love my ba-by like the fin-est w, wine. _

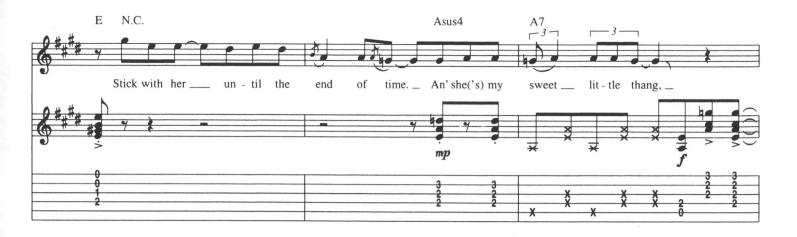

Stick with her ___ un-til the end of time. ___ An' she('s) my sweet ___ lit-tle thang, ___

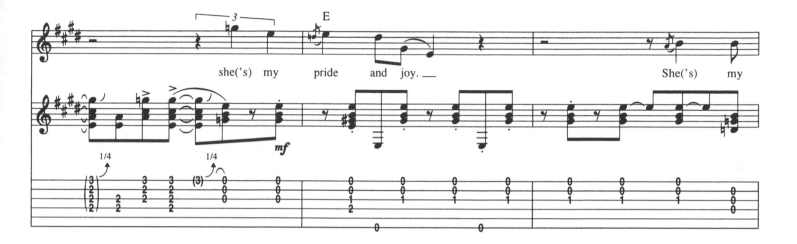

she('s) my pride and joy. ___ She('s) my

sweet lit-tle ba-by, I'm ___ her ___ lit-tle lov-er boy. ___

Verse

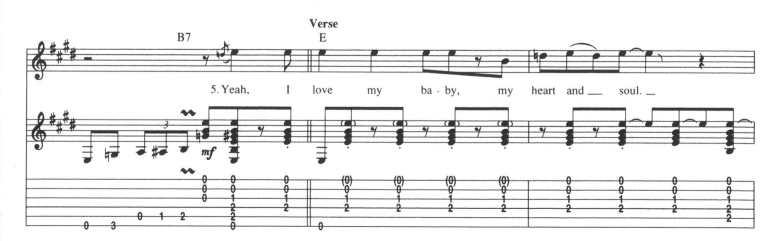

5. Yeah, I love my ba-by, my heart and ___ soul. ___

Love like ___ ours ah, won't ___ nev - er grow ___ old. ___ She('s) my sweet ___ lit - tle thang, ___

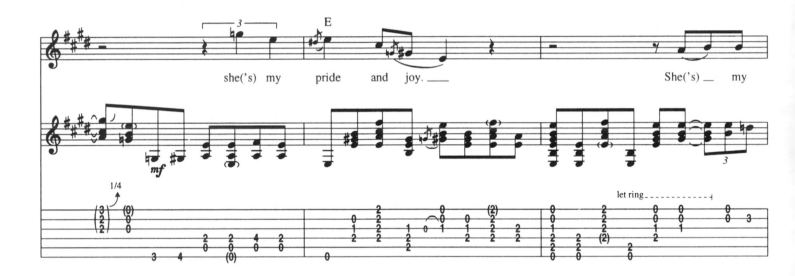

she('s) my pride and joy. ___ She('s) ___ my

sweet lit-tle ba - by, I'm ___ her ___ lit - tle lov - er boy. ___

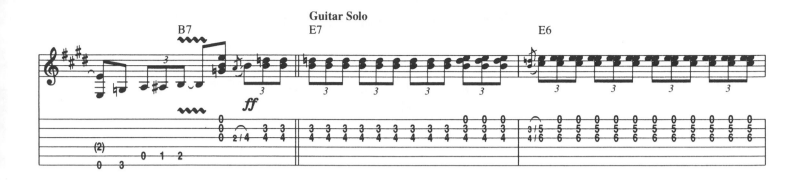

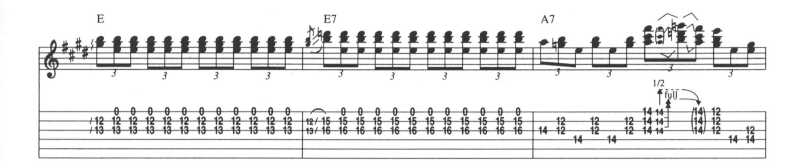

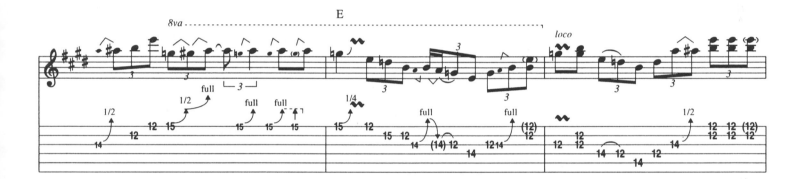

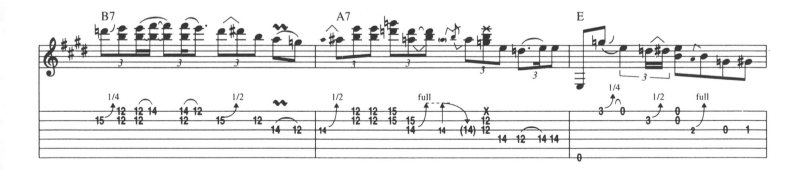

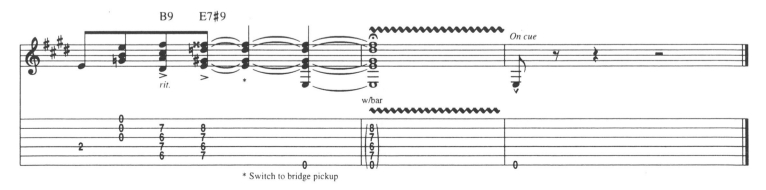

* Switch to bridge pickup

Satisfy Susie

Words and Music by Lonnie McIntosh and Tim Drummond

† Gtrs. 1 & 2;
Tune Down 1 Step, Capo III:

① = D   ④ = C
② = A   ⑤ = G
③ = F   ⑥ = D

Gtr. 3; Tune Down 1/2 Step:

① = Eb   ④ = Db
② = Bb   ⑤ = Ab
③ = Gb   ⑥ = Eb

Intro
Moderately ♩ = 135

* Symbols in parentheses represent chord names respective to capoed guitar and do not reflect actual sounding chords. Capoed fret is "0" in TAB.

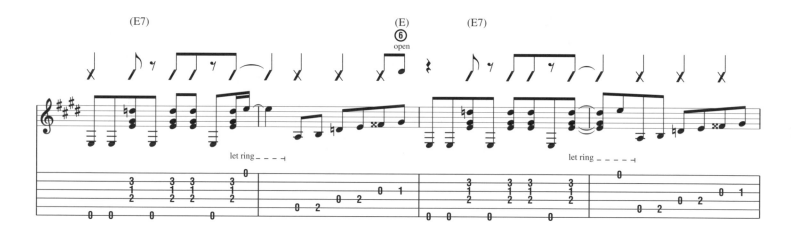

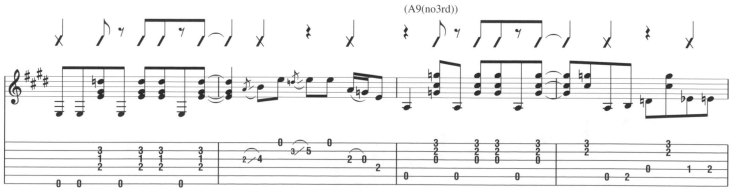

† Editor's note: You can accomplish the same result without tuning down a whole step by remaining in standard tuning and capoing at the first fret.

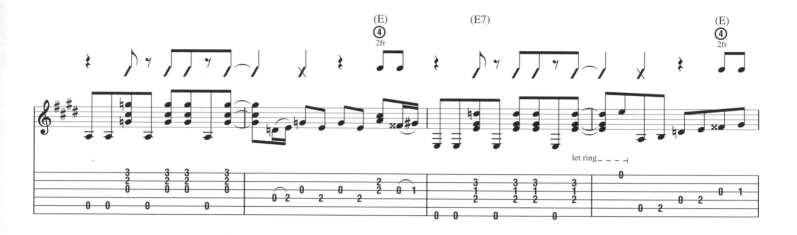

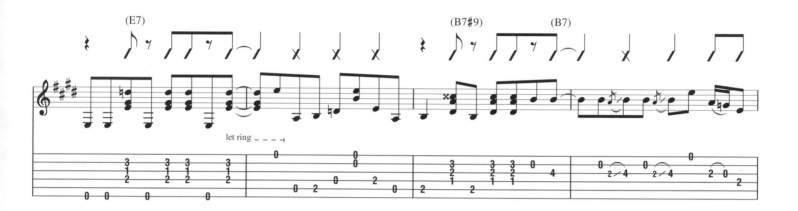

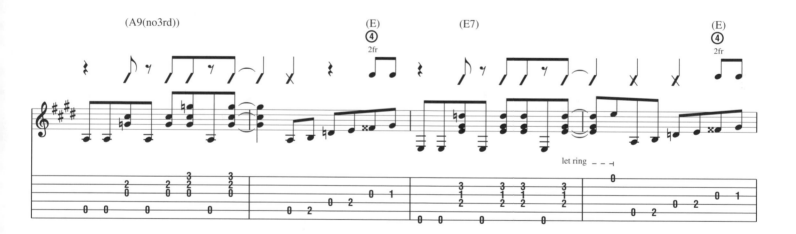

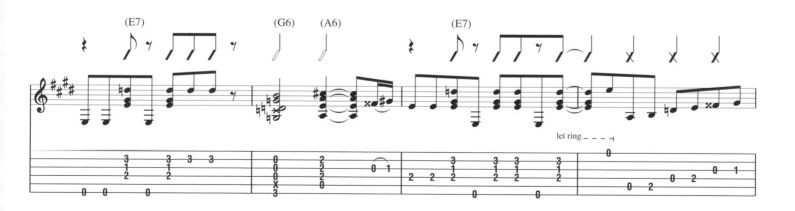

Verse

1. Can I tell ya 'bout my ba - by, she's
2., 3., 4. *See Additional Lyrics*

ev - 'ry man's dream? She could be the fold - out in a gir - ly ma - ga - zine. I got to

Chorus

sat - is - fy Su - sie.
(You got to sat - is - fy Su - sie.
I got to sa - tis - fy Su - sie.

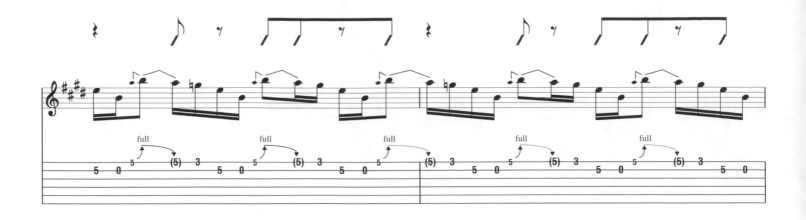

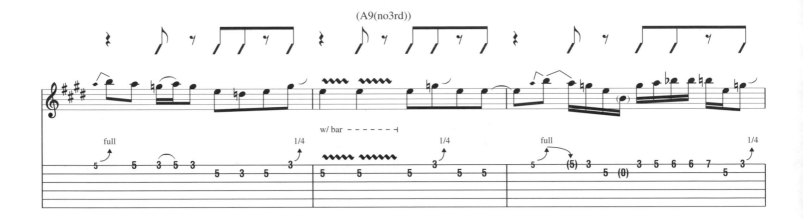

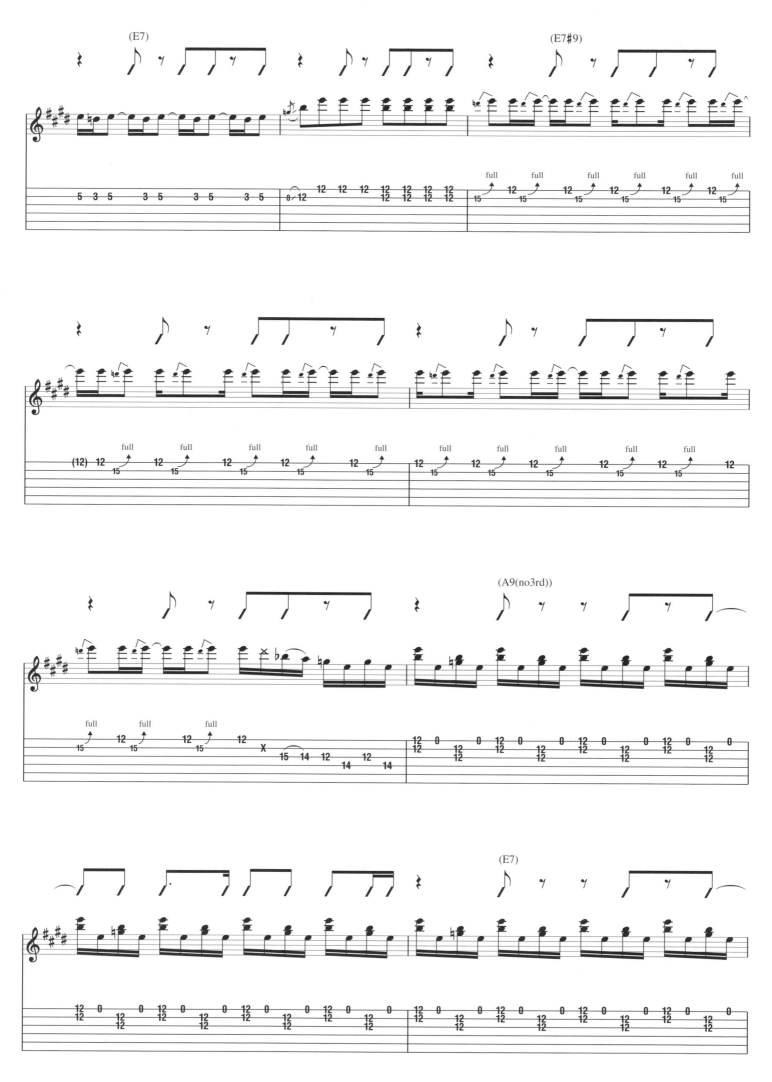

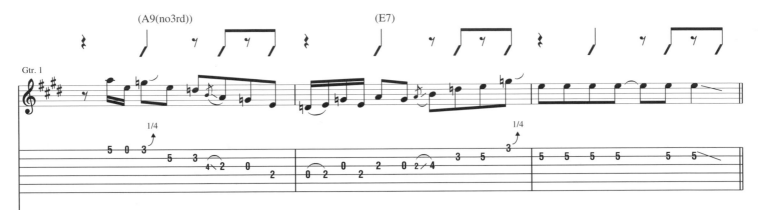

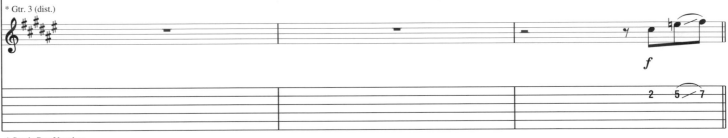

* Stevie Ray Vaughan

Guitar Solo

Gtr. 1: w/ Riff A, simile
Gtr. 2 tacet

** Symbols in parentheses represent chord names respective to capoed guitar.
Symbols above reflect actual sounding chords. Chord symbols reflect implied harmony.

Gtr. 1: w/ Riff B, 1st 6 meas., simile

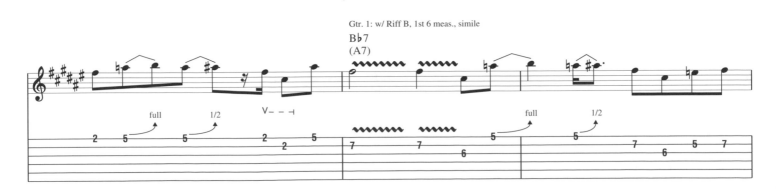

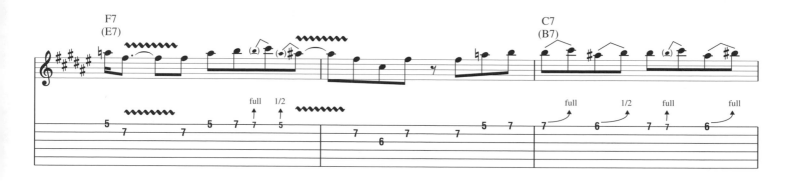

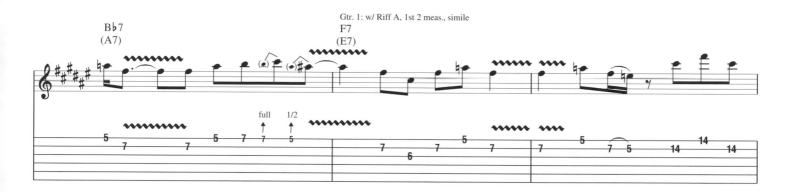

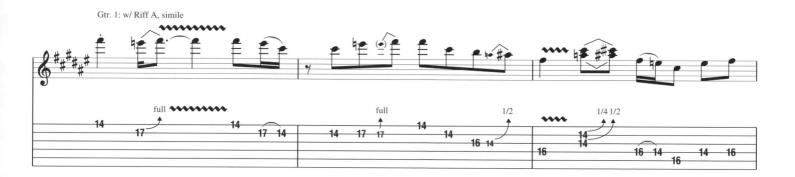

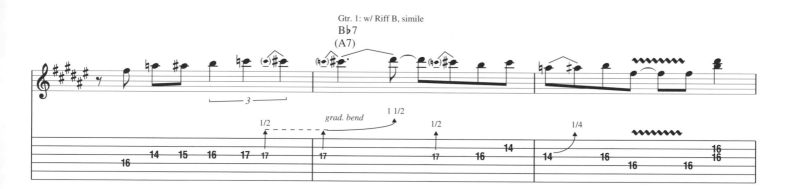

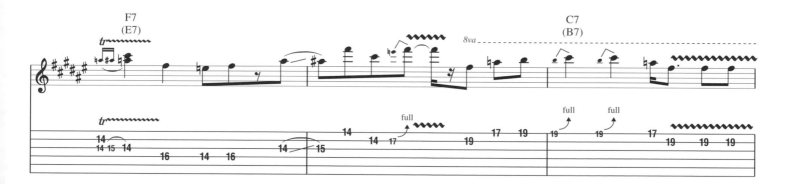

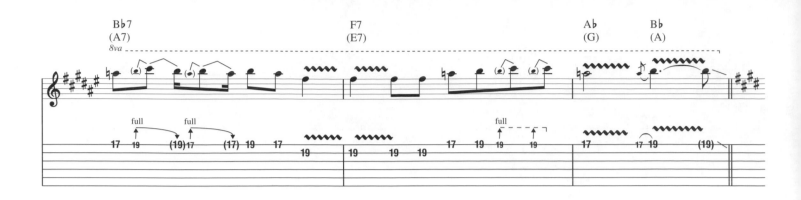

Interlude

Gtr. 3 tacet

D.S. al Coda
(take repeat)

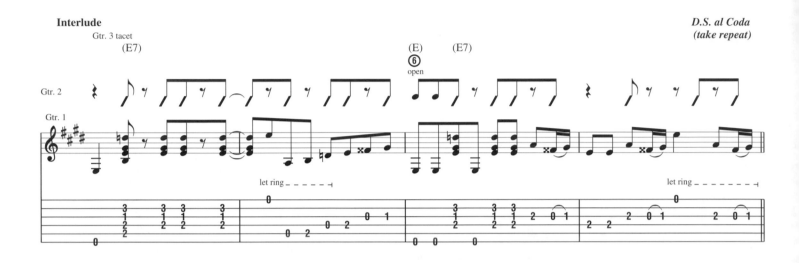

⊕ *Coda*

Interlude

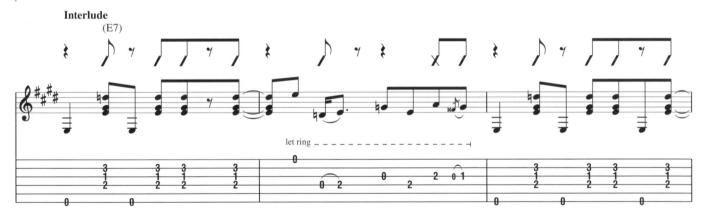

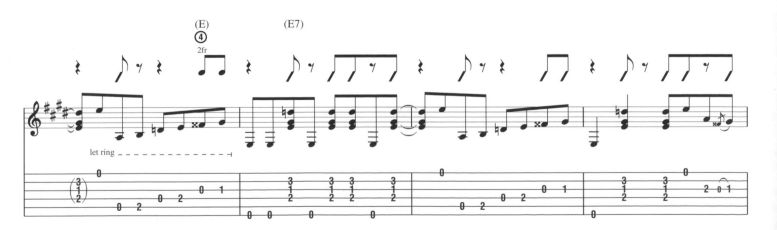

Additional Lyrics

2. Bought a brand new Chevy,
   Keep it shined up in the drive.
   Souped up to the limit
   'Cause Susie likes to fly it.

3. Susie's into lovin'
   Anyway you can.
   She don't give her lovin'
   To any other man.

4. You ask me if I'm happy,
   Do I look satisfied?
   Susie's got the way to keep
   The twinkle in my eye.

The Sky Is Crying

Words and Music by Elmore James

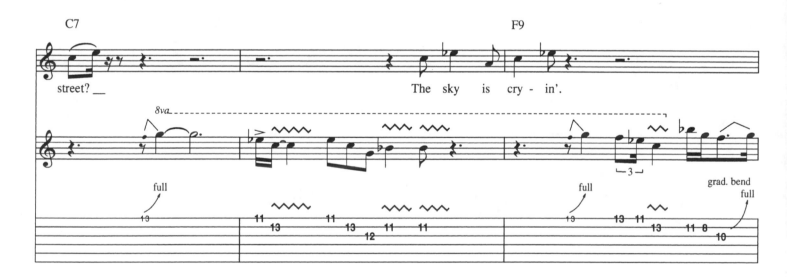

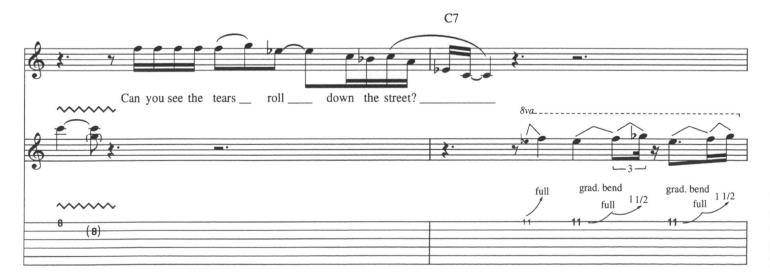

street.

You know it

hurt me, hurt me so bad, _____ made my poor heart, uh, skip a beat. _____

C Guitar solo

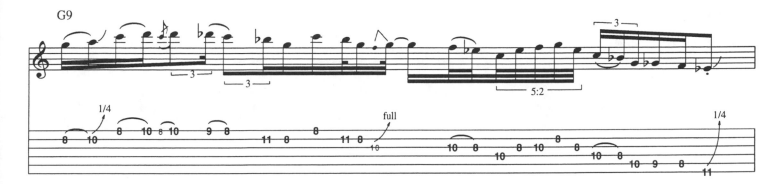

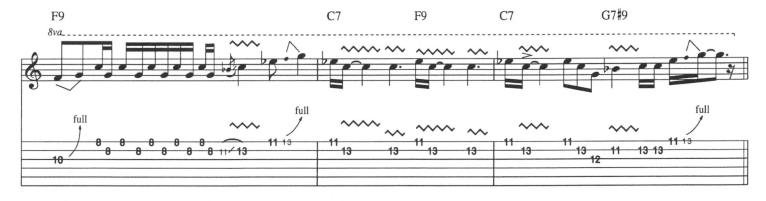

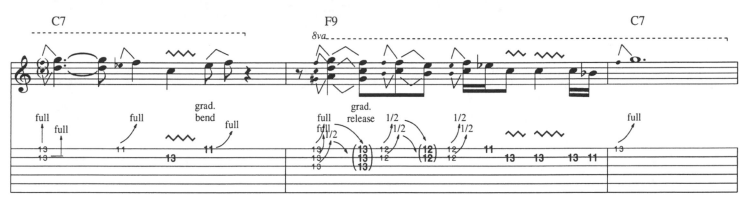

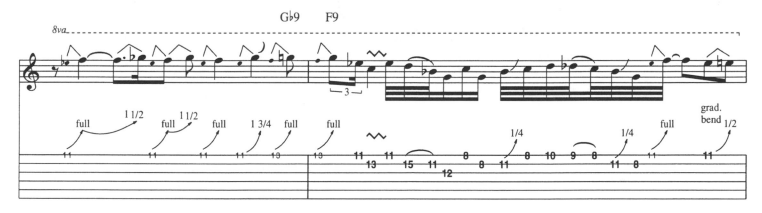

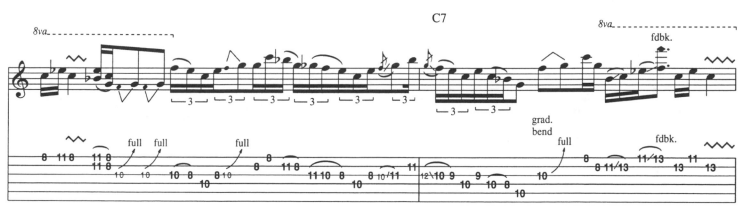

that my ba-by don't _____ love me no more.

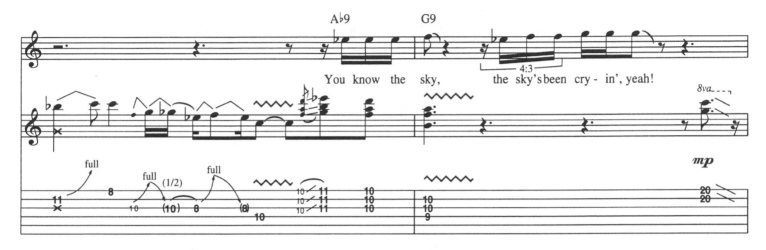

You know the sky, the sky's been cry-in', yeah!

Can you see the tears ____ roll-in' down my nose?

Smoking Gun

Written by Bruce Bromberg, Richard Cousins and Robert Cray

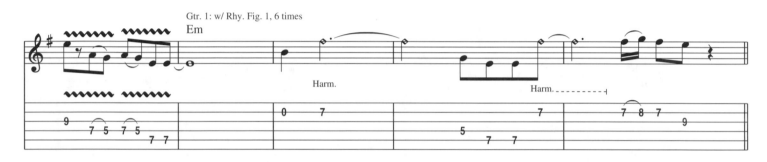

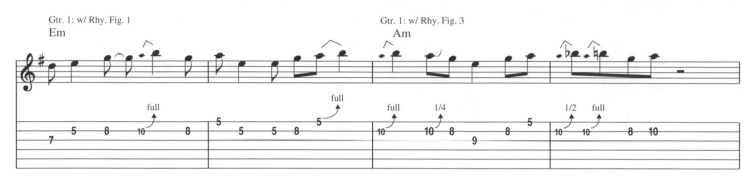

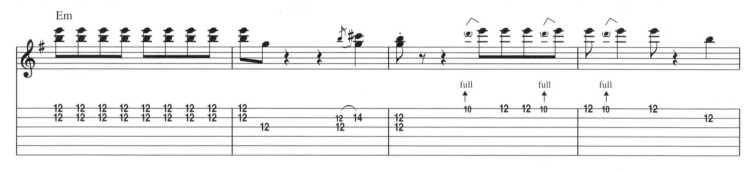

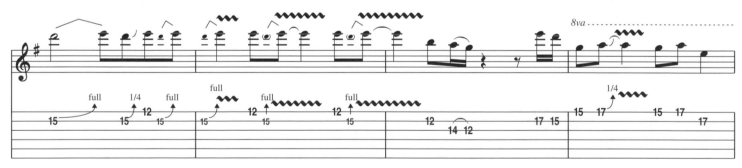

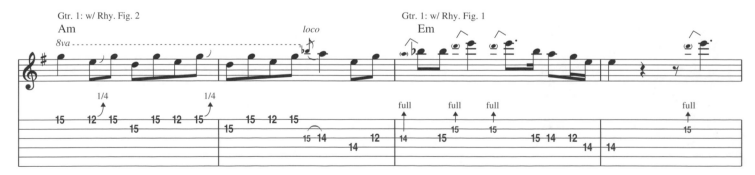

Em

They've knocked me down, and tak-en it. Oh.

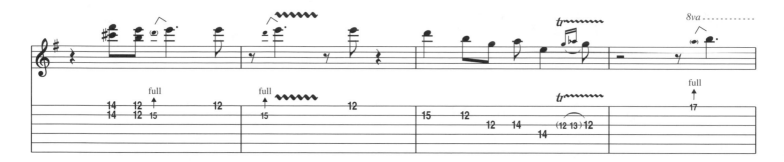

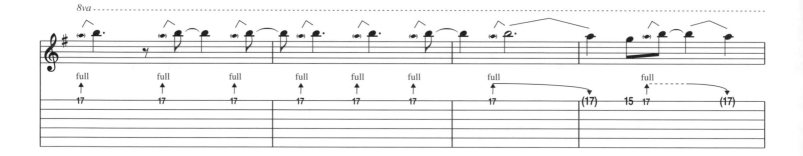

Fade

Verse

I'm standing here bewildered,
I can't remember just what I've done.
I can hear the sirens whining,
My eyes blinded by the sun.
I know that I should be running,
My heart's beating just like a drum.
Now they've knocked me down and taken it,
That still hot smokin' gun.

Sweet Little Angel

Words and Music by B.B. King and Jules Bihari

* Chord symbols reflect overall tonality.

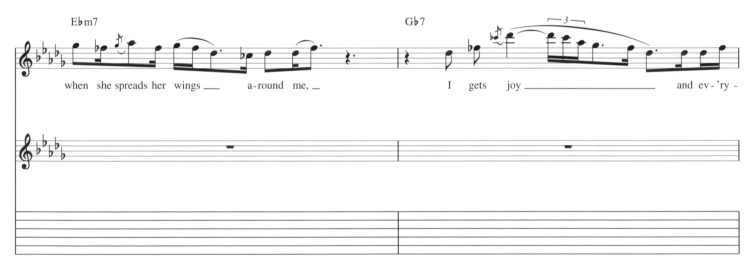

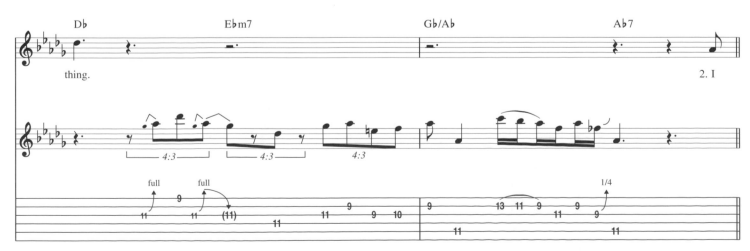

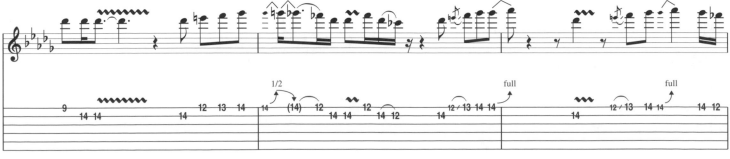

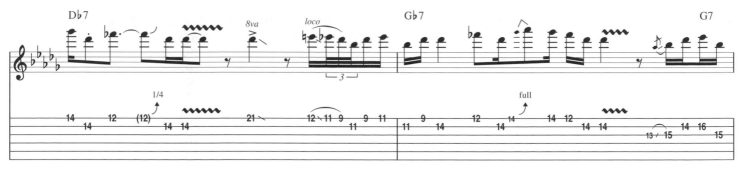

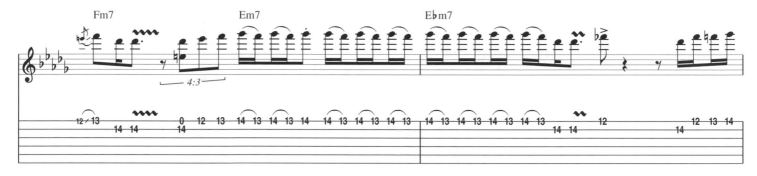

D.S. al Coda

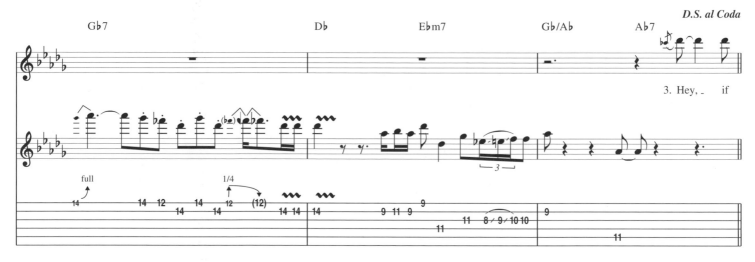

3. Hey, ___ if

⊕ *Coda*

Free Time

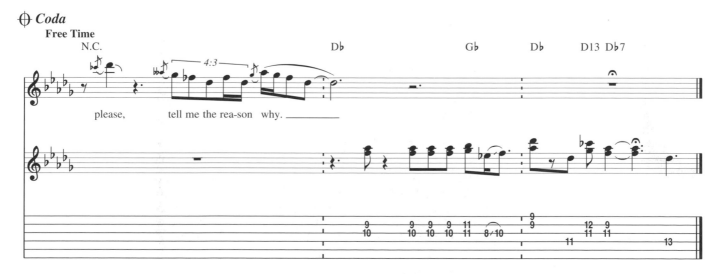

please, ___ tell me the rea-son why. ___

The Things That I Used to Do

Words and Music by Eddie "Guitar Slim" Jones

* Symbols in parentheses represent chord names respective to capoed guitar. Symbols above reflect actual sounding chord.

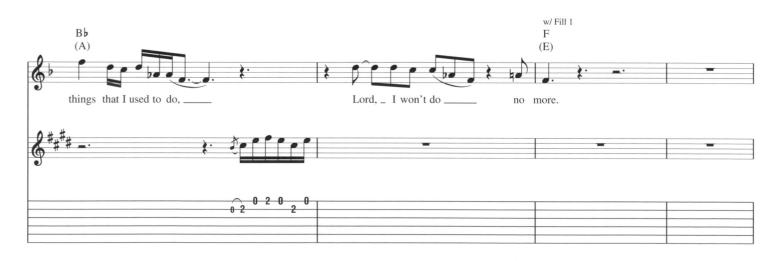

w/ Fill 2, 2nd time

C7
(B7)

Bb7
(A7)

I used to set and hold   your hand, ba - by,   cry, _____ beg-gin' you not to go. ___

w/ Fill 2, 2nd time

F
(E)

|1.

C7
(B7)

|2.

C7
(B7)

Turnaround:

Solo

F
(E)

Bb
(A)

F
(E)

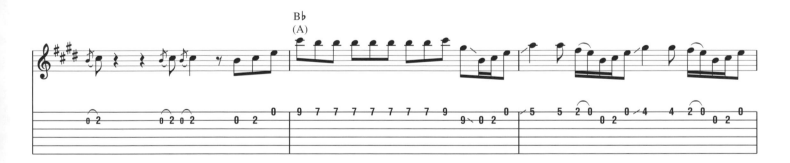

Bb
(A)

Fill 2

Fill 3

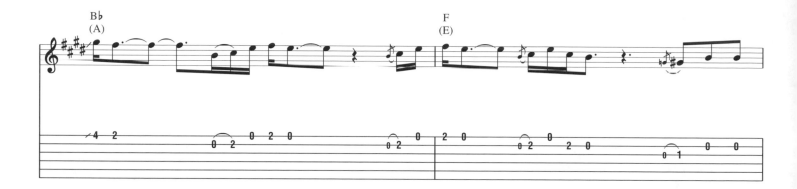

D.S. al Coda

I'm go-ing to send   you back to your

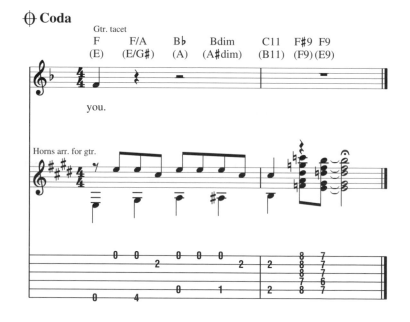

⊕ **Coda**

you.

Additional Lyrics

2. I would search all night for you, baby,
   Lord, and my search would always end in vain.
   I would search all night for you, baby,
   Lord, and my search would always end in vain.
   But I knew all along, darlin',
   That you was hid out with your other man.

3. I'm going to send you back to your mother, baby,
   Lord, and I'm going back to my family too.
   I'm going to send you back to your mother, baby,
   Lord, and I'm going back to my family too.
   'Cause nothing I do that please you, baby,
   Lord, I just can't get along with you.

Wayfaring Pilgrim

Written by Roy Buchanan and Ed Freeman

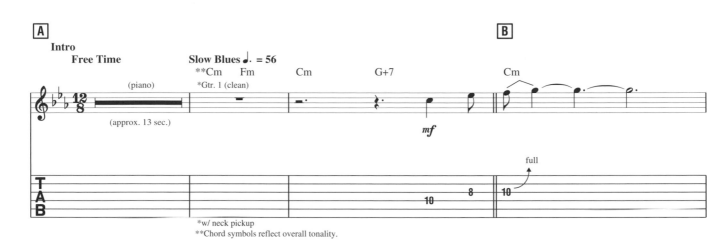

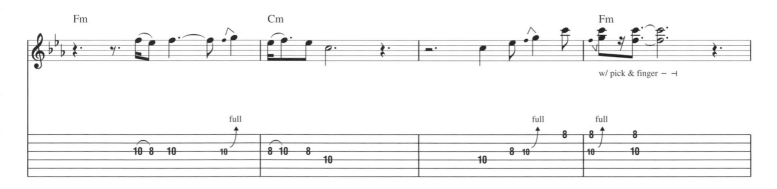

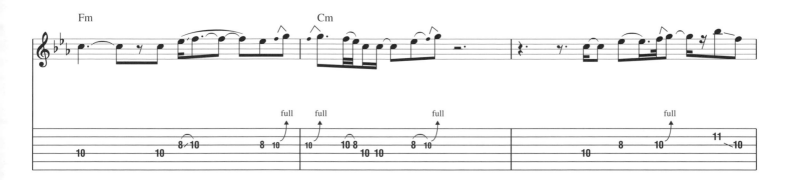

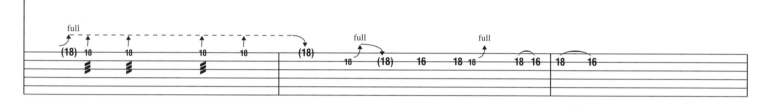

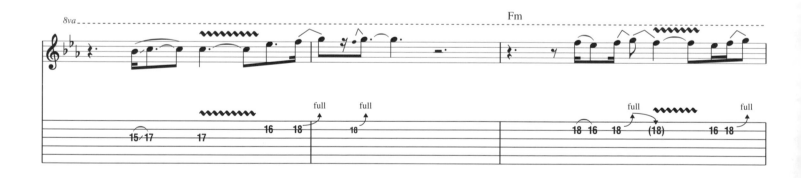

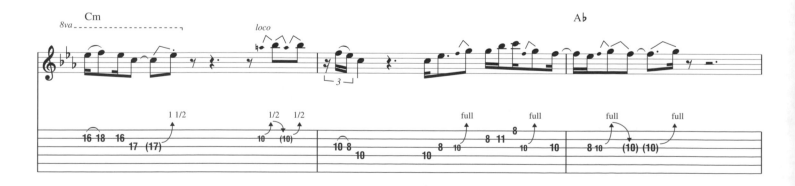

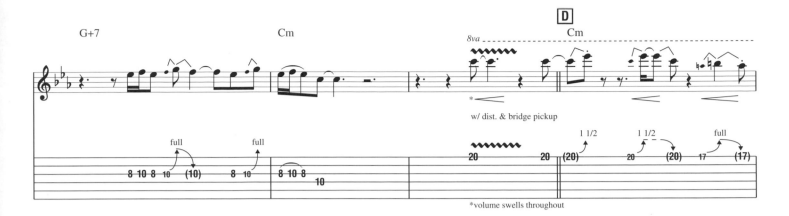

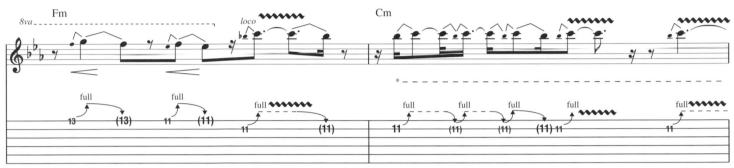

*volume swells throughout

*Manipulate tone control in same manner as vol. swells.

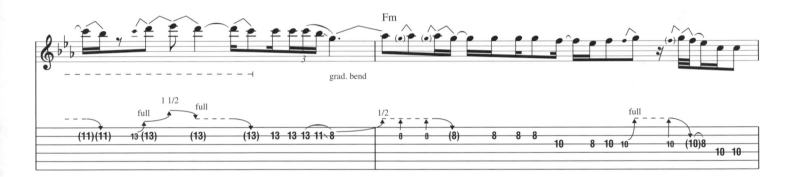

grad. bend

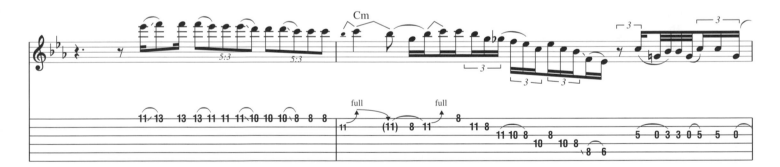

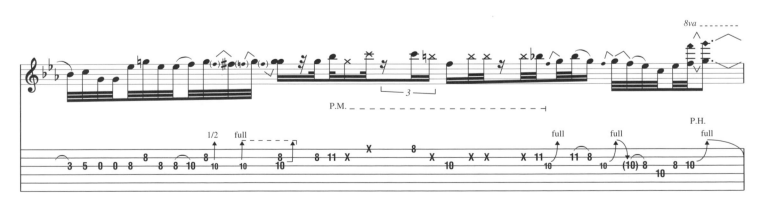

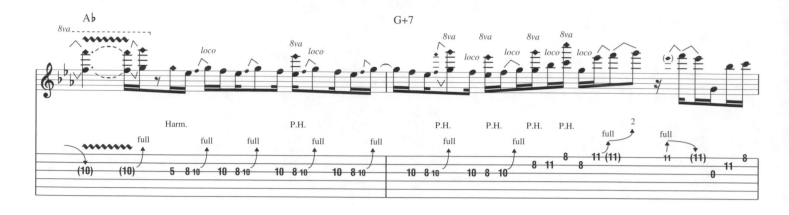

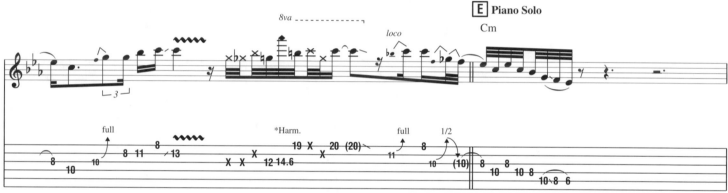

*Located between 14th and 15th fret.

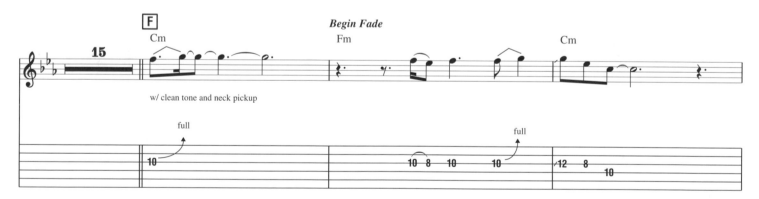

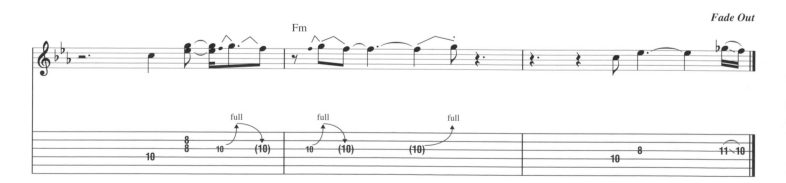

You Upset Me Baby

Words and Music by B.B. King and Jules Bihari

*Chord symbols reflect basic harmony.

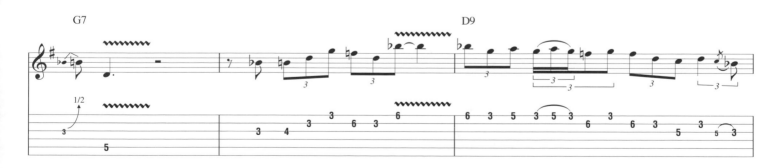

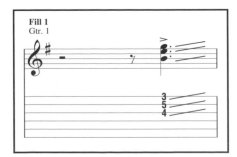

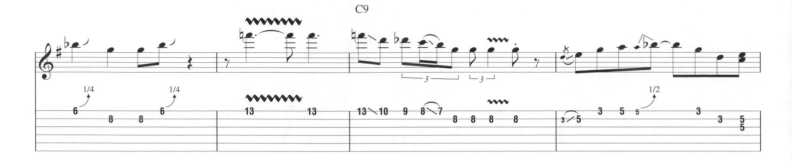

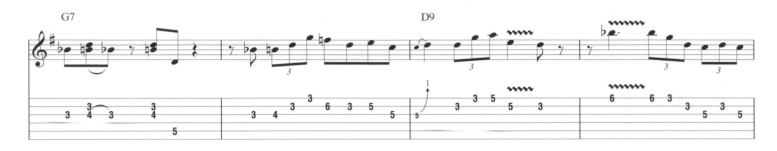

Saxophone Solo
Gtr. 1: comp ad lib.
Gtr. 2 tacet

D.S. al Coda

4. Well,   I've

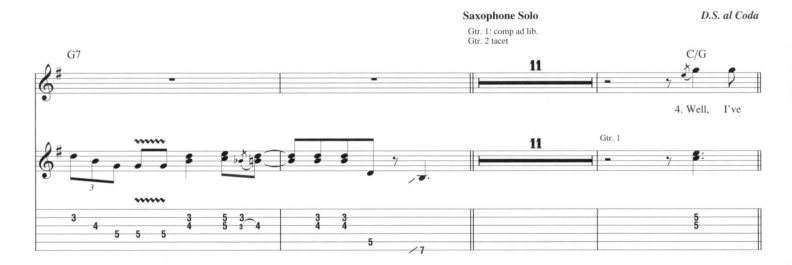

Coda

tree,   wom - an, what you   do to   me. __

Guitar Notation Legend

Guitar music can be notated three different ways: on a *musical staff*, in *tablature*, and in *rhythm slashes*.

RHYTHM SLASHES are written above the staff. Strum chords in the rhythm indicated. Use the chord diagrams found at the top of the first page of the transcription for the appropriate chord voicings. Round noteheads indicate single notes.

THE MUSICAL STAFF shows pitches and rhythms and is divided by bar lines into measures. Pitches are named after the first seven letters of the alphabet.

TABLATURE graphically represents the guitar fingerboard. Each horizontal line represents a string, and each number represents a fret.

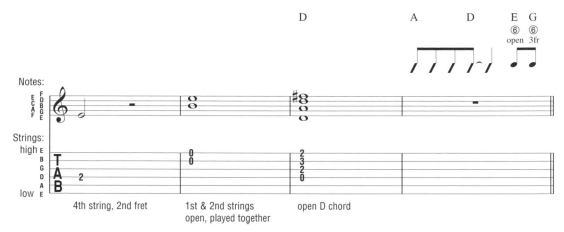

4th string, 2nd fret   1st & 2nd strings open, played together   open D chord

Definitions for Special Guitar Notation

HALF-STEP BEND: Strike the note and bend up 1/2 step.

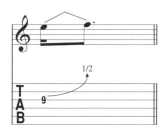

WHOLE-STEP BEND: Strike the note and bend up one step.

GRACE NOTE BEND: Strike the note and immediately bend up as indicated.

SLIGHT (MICROTONE) BEND: Strike the note and bend up 1/4 step.

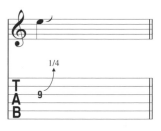

BEND AND RELEASE: Strike the note and bend up as indicated, then release back to the original note. Only the first note is struck.

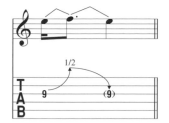

PRE-BEND: Bend the note as indicated, then strike it.

PRE-BEND AND RELEASE: Bend the note as indicated. Strike it and release the bend back to the original note.

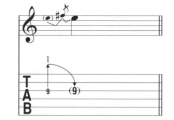

UNISON BEND: Strike the two notes simultaneously and bend the lower note up to the pitch of the higher.

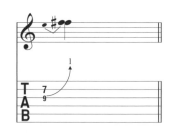

VIBRATO: The string is vibrated by rapidly bending and releasing the note with the fretting hand.

WIDE VIBRATO: The pitch is varied to a greater degree by vibrating with the fretting hand.

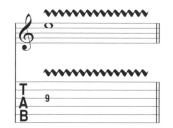

HAMMER-ON: Strike the first (lower) note with one finger, then sound the higher note (on the same string) with another finger by fretting it without picking.

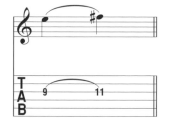

PULL-OFF: Place both fingers on the notes to be sounded. Strike the first note and without picking, pull the finger off to sound the second (lower) note.

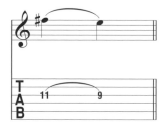

LEGATO SLIDE: Strike the first note and then slide the same fret-hand finger up or down to the second note. The second note is not struck.

SHIFT SLIDE: Same as legato slide, except the second note is struck.

TRILL: Very rapidly alternate between the notes indicated by continuously hammering on and pulling off.

TAPPING: Hammer ("tap") the fret indicated with the pick-hand index or middle finger and pull off to the note fretted by the fret hand.

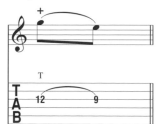

NATURAL HARMONIC: Strike the note while the fret-hand lightly touches the string directly over the fret indicated.

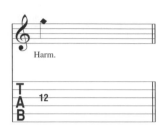

PINCH HARMONIC: The note is fretted normally and a harmonic is produced by adding the edge of the thumb or the tip of the index finger of the pick hand to the normal pick attack.

HARP HARMONIC: The note is fretted normally and a harmonic is produced by gently resting the pick hand's index finger directly above the indicated fret (in parentheses) while the pick hand's thumb or pick assists by plucking the appropriate string.

PICK SCRAPE: The edge of the pick is rubbed down (or up) the string, producing a scratchy sound.

MUFFLED STRINGS: A percussive sound is produced by laying the fret hand across the string(s) without depressing, and striking them with the pick hand.

PALM MUTING: The note is partially muted by the pick hand lightly touching the string(s) just before the bridge.

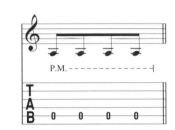

RAKE: Drag the pick across the strings indicated with a single motion.

TREMOLO PICKING: The note is picked as rapidly and continuously as possible.

ARPEGGIATE: Play the notes of the chord indicated by quickly rolling them from bottom to top.

VIBRATO BAR DIVE AND RETURN: The pitch of the note or chord is dropped a specified number of steps (in rhythm), then returned to the original pitch.

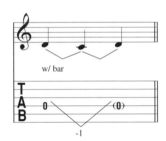

VIBRATO BAR SCOOP: Depress the bar just before striking the note, then quickly release the bar.

VIBRATO BAR DIP: Strike the note and then immediately drop a specified number of steps, then release back to the original pitch.

Additional Musical Definitions

> (accent)	• Accentuate note (play it louder).	
^ (accent)	• Accentuate note with great intensity.	
(staccato)	• Play the note short.	
⊓	• Downstroke	
V	• Upstroke	
D.S. al Coda	• Go back to the sign (𝄋), then play until the measure marked "*To Coda*," then skip to the section labelled "**Coda**."	
D.C. al Fine	• Go back to the beginning of the song and play until the measure marked "*Fine*" (end).	

Rhy. Fig. • Label used to recall a recurring accompaniment pattern (usually chordal).

Riff • Label used to recall composed, melodic lines (usually single notes) which recur.

Fill • Label used to identify a brief melodic figure which is to be inserted into the arrangement.

Rhy. Fill • A chordal version of a Fill.

tacet • Instrument is silent (drops out).

• Repeat measures between signs.

• When a repeated section has different endings, play the first ending only the first time and the second ending only the second time.

NOTE: Tablature numbers in parentheses mean:
1. The note is being sustained over a system (note in standard notation is tied), or
2. The note is sustained, but a new articulation (such as a hammer-on, pull-off, slide or vibrato) begins, or
3. The note is a barely audible "ghost" note (note in standard notation is also in parentheses).

RECORDED VERSIONS®
The Best Note-For-Note Transcriptions Available

ALL BOOKS INCLUDE TABLATURE

692015	Aerosmith – Greatest Hits	$22.95
690603	Aerosmith – O Yeah! (Ultimate Hits)	$24.95
690178	Alice in Chains – Acoustic	$19.95
694865	Alice in Chains – Dirt	$19.95
690387	Alice in Chains – Nothing Safe: The Best of the Box	$19.95
690812	All American Rejects – Move Along	$19.95
694932	Allman Brothers Band – Volume 1	$24.95
694933	Allman Brothers Band – Volume 2	$24.95
694934	Allman Brothers Band – Volume 3	$24.95
690865	Atreyu – A Deathgrip on Yesterday	$19.95
690609	Audioslave	$19.95
690804	Audioslave – Out of Exile	$19.95
690884	Audioslave – Revelations	$19.95
690820	Avenged Sevenfold – City of Evil	$22.95
690366	Bad Company – Original Anthology, Book 1	$19.95
690503	Beach Boys – Very Best of	$19.95
690489	Beatles – 1	$24.95
694929	Beatles – 1962-1966	$24.95
694930	Beatles – 1967-1970	$24.95
694832	Beatles – For Acoustic Guitar	$22.95
690110	Beatles – White Album (Book 1)	$19.95
692385	Chuck Berry	$19.95
690835	Billy Talent	$19.95
692200	Black Sabbath – We Sold Our Soul for Rock 'N' Roll	$19.95
690674	blink-182	$19.95
690831	blink-182 – Greatest Hits	$19.95
690491	David Bowie – Best of	$19.95
690873	Breaking Benjamin – Phobia	$19.95
690764	Breaking Benjamin – We Are Not Alone	$19.95
690451	Jeff Buckley – Collection	$24.95
690590	Eric Clapton – Anthology	$29.95
690415	Clapton Chronicles – Best of Eric Clapton	$18.95
690074	Eric Clapton – The Cream of Clapton	$24.95
690716	Eric Clapton – Me and Mr. Johnson	$19.95
694869	Eric Clapton – Unplugged	$22.95
690162	The Clash – Best of	$19.95
690828	Coheed & Cambria – Good Apollo I'm Burning Star, IV, Vol. 1: From Fear Through the Eyes of Madness	$19.95
690593	Coldplay – A Rush of Blood to the Head	$19.95
690838	Cream – Royal Albert Hall: London May 2-3-5-6 2005	$22.95
690856	Creed – Greatest Hits	$22.95
690401	Creed – Human Clay	$19.95
690819	Creedence Clearwater Revival – Best of	$19.95
690572	Steve Cropper – Soul Man	$19.95
690613	Crosby, Stills & Nash – Best of	$19.95
690289	Deep Purple – Best of	$17.95
690784	Def Leppard – Best of	$19.95
690347	The Doors – Anthology	$22.95
690348	The Doors – Essential Guitar Collection	$16.95
690810	Fall Out Boy – From Under the Cork Tree	$19.95
690664	Fleetwood Mac – Best of	$19.95
690870	Flyleaf	$19.95
690808	Foo Fighters – In Your Honor	$19.95
690805	Robben Ford – Best of	$19.95
694920	Free – Best of	$19.95
690848	Godsmack – IV	$19.95
690601	Good Charlotte – The Young and the Hopeless	$19.95
690697	Jim Hall – Best of	$19.95
690840	Ben Harper – Both Sides of the Gun	$19.95
694798	George Harrison – Anthology	$19.95
692930	Jimi Hendrix – Are You Experienced?	$24.95

00692931	Jimi Hendrix – Axis: Bold As Love	$22.95
00690608	Jimi Hendrix – Blue Wild Angel	$24.95
00692932	Jimi Hendrix – Electric Ladyland	$24.95
00690017	Jimi Hendrix – Live at Woodstock	$24.95
00690602	Jimi Hendrix – Smash Hits	$19.95
00690843	H.I.M. – Dark Light	$19.95
00690869	Hinder – Extreme Behavior	$19.95
00690692	Billy Idol – Very Best of	$19.95
00690688	Incubus – A Crow Left of the Murder	$19.95
00690457	Incubus – Make Yourself	$19.95
00690544	Incubus – Morningview	$19.95
00690790	Iron Maiden Anthology	$24.95
00690730	Alan Jackson – Guitar Collection	$19.95
00690721	Jet – Get Born	$19.95
00690684	Jethro Tull – Aqualung	$19.95
00690647	Jewel – Best of	$19.95
00690814	John5 – Songs for Sanity	$19.95
00690751	John5 – Vertigo	$19.95
00690845	Eric Johnson – Bloom	$19.95
00690846	Jack Johnson and Friends – Sing-A-Longs and Lullabies for the Film Curious George	$19.95
00690271	Robert Johnson – New Transcriptions	$24.95
00699131	Janis Joplin – Best of	$19.95
00690427	Judas Priest – Best of	$19.95
00690742	The Killers – Hot Fuss	$19.95
00694903	Kiss – Best of	$24.95
00690780	Korn – Greatest Hits, Volume 1	$22.95
00690834	Lamb of God – Ashes of the Wake	$19.95
00690875	Lamb of God – Sacrament	$19.95
00690823	Ray LaMontagne – Trouble	$19.95
00690679	John Lennon – Guitar Collection	$19.95
00690781	Linkin Park – Hybrid Theory	$22.95
00690782	Linkin Park – Meteora	$22.95
00690783	Live – Best of	$19.95
00690743	Los Lonely Boys	$19.95
00690876	Los Lonely Boys – Sacred	$19.95
00690720	Lostprophets – Start Something	$19.95
00694954	Lynyrd Skynyrd – New Best of	$19.95
00690752	Lynyrd Skynyrd – Street Survivors	$19.95
00690577	Yngwie Malmsteen – Anthology	$24.95
00690754	Marilyn Manson – Lest We Forget	$19.95
00694956	Bob Marley – Legend	$19.95
00694945	Bob Marley – Songs of Freedom	$24.95
00690657	Maroon5 – Songs About Jane	$19.95
00120080	Don McLean – Songbook	$19.95
00694951	Megadeth – Rust in Peace	$22.95
00690768	Megadeth – The System Has Failed	$19.95
00690505	John Mellencamp – Guitar Collection	$19.95
00690646	Pat Metheny – One Quiet Night	$19.95
00690558	Pat Metheny – Trio: 99>00	$19.95
00690040	Steve Miller Band – Young Hearts	$19.95
00690794	Mudvayne – Lost and Found	$19.95
00690611	Nirvana	$22.95
00694883	Nirvana – Nevermind	$19.95
00690026	Nirvana – Unplugged in New York	$19.95
00690807	The Offspring – Greatest Hits	$19.95
00694847	Ozzy Osbourne – Best of	$22.95
00690399	Ozzy Osbourne – Ozzman Cometh	$19.95
00690866	Panic! At the Disco – A Fever You Can't Sweat Out	$19.95
00694855	Pearl Jam – Ten	$19.95
00690439	A Perfect Circle – Mer De Noms	$19.95
00690661	A Perfect Circle – Thirteenth Step	$19.95
00690499	Tom Petty – Definitive Guitar Collection	$19.95
00690428	Pink Floyd – Dark Side of the Moon	$19.95
00690789	Poison – Best of	$19.95
00693864	The Police – Best of	$19.95

00694975	Queen – Greatest Hits	$24.95
00690670	Queensryche – Very Best of	$19.95
00690878	The Raconteurs – Broken Boy Soldiers	$19.95
00694910	Rage Against the Machine	$19.95
00690055	Red Hot Chili Peppers – Blood Sugar Sex Magik	$19.95
00690584	Red Hot Chili Peppers – By the Way	$19.95
00690379	Red Hot Chili Peppers – Californication	$19.95
00690673	Red Hot Chili Peppers – Greatest Hits	$19.95
00690852	Red Hot Chili Peppers – Stadium Arcadium	$24.95
00690511	Django Reinhardt – Definitive Collection	$19.95
00690779	Relient K – MMHMM	$19.95
00690643	Relient K – Two Lefts Don't Make a Right...But Three Do	$19.95
00690631	Rolling Stones – Guitar Anthology	$24.95
00690685	David Lee Roth – Eat 'Em and Smile	$19.95
00690694	David Lee Roth – Guitar Anthology	$24.95
00690031	Santana's Greatest Hits	$19.95
00690796	Michael Schenker – Very Best of	$19.95
00690566	Scorpions – Best of	$19.95
00690604	Bob Seger – Guitar Collection	$19.95
00690803	Kenny Wayne Shepherd Band – Best of	$19.95
00690857	Shinedown – Us and Them	$19.95
00690530	Slipknot – Iowa	$19.95
00690733	Slipknot – Vol. 3 (The Subliminal Verses)	$19.95
00120004	Steely Dan – Best of	$24.95
00694921	Steppenwolf – Best of	$22.95
00690655	Mike Stern – Best of	$19.95
00690877	Stone Sour – Come What(ever) May	$19.95
00690520	Styx Guitar Collection	$19.95
00120081	Sublime	$19.95
00690771	SUM 41 – Chuck	$19.95
00690767	Switchfoot – The Beautiful Letdown	$19.95
00690830	System of a Down – Hypnotize	$19.95
00690799	System of a Down – Mezmerize	$19.95
00690531	System of a Down – Toxicity	$19.95
00694824	James Taylor – Best of	$16.95
00690871	Three Days Grace – One-X	$19.95
00690737	3 Doors Down – The Better Life	$22.95
00690683	Robin Trower – Bridge of Sighs	$19.95
00690740	Shania Twain – Guitar Collection	$19.95
00699191	U2 – Best of: 1980-1990	$19.95
00690732	U2 – Best of: 1990-2000	$19.95
00690775	U2 – How to Dismantle an Atomic Bomb	$22.95
00690575	Steve Vai – Alive in an Ultra World	$22.95
00660137	Steve Vai – Passion & Warfare	$24.95
00690116	Stevie Ray Vaughan – Guitar Collection	$24.95
00660058	Stevie Ray Vaughan – Lightnin' Blues 1983-1987	$24.95
00694835	Stevie Ray Vaughan – The Sky Is Crying	$22.95
00690015	Stevie Ray Vaughan – Texas Flood	$19.95
00690772	Velvet Revolver – Contraband	$22.95
00690071	Weezer (The Blue Album)	$19.95
00690447	The Who – Best of	$24.95
00690589	ZZ Top Guitar Anthology	$22.95

GUITAR BIBLES

from **HAL•LEONARD**®

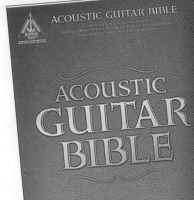

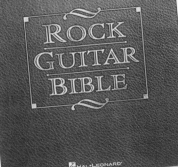

Hal Leonard proudly presents the Guitar Bible series. Each volume contains great songs in authentic, note-for-note transcriptions with lyrics and tablature.

ACOUSTIC GUITAR BIBLE

35 acoustic classics: Angie • Building a Mystery • Change the World • Dust in the Wind • Hold My Hand • Iris • Maggie May • Southern Cross • Tears in Heaven • Wild World • and more.
00690432 .... $19.95

ACOUSTIC ROCK GUITAR BIBLE

35 classics: And I Love Her • Behind Blue Eyes • Come to My Window • Free Fallin' • Give a Little Bit • More Than Words • Night Moves • Pink Houses • Slide • 3 AM • and more.
00690625 .... $19.95

BABY BOOMER'S GUITAR BIBLE

35 songs: Angie • Can't Buy Me Love • Happy Together • Hey Jude • Imagine • Laughing • Longer • My Girl • New Kid in Town • Rebel, Rebel • Wild Thing • and more.
00690412 .... $19.95

BLUES GUITAR BIBLE

35 blues tunes: Boom Boom • Hide Away • I Can't Quit You Baby • I'm Your Hoochie Coochie Man • Killing Floor • Pride and Joy • Sweet Little Angel • The Thrill Is Gone • and more.
00690437 .... $19.95

BLUES-ROCK GUITAR BIBLE

35 songs: Cross Road Blues (Crossroads) • Hide Away • The House Is Rockin' • Love Struck Baby • Move It On Over • Piece of My Heart • Statesboro Blues • You Shook Me • more.
00690450 .... $19.95

CLASSIC ROCK GUITAR BIBLE

33 essential rock songs: Beast of Burden • Cat Scratch Fever • Double Vision • Free Ride • Hard to Handle • Life in the Fast Lane • The Stroke • Won't Get Fooled Again • and more.
00690662 .... $19.95

COUNTRY GUITAR BIBLE

35 country classics: Ain't Goin' Down • Blue Eyes Crying in the Rain • Boot Scootin' Boogie • Friends in Low Places • I'm So Lonesome I Could Cry • T-R-O-U-B-L-E • and more.
00690465 .... $19.95

DISCO GUITAR BIBLE

30 stand-out songs from the disco days: Brick House • Disco Inferno • Funkytown • Get Down Tonight • I Love the Night Life • Le Freak • Stayin' Alive • Y.M.C.A. • and more.
00690627 .... $17.95

EARLY ROCK GUITAR BIBLE

35 fantastic classics: Blue Suede Shoes • Do Wah Diddy Diddy • Hang On Sloopy • I'm a Believer • Louie, Louie • Oh, Pretty Woman • Surfin' U.S.A. • Twist and Shout • and more.
00690680 .... $17.95

FOLK-ROCK GUITAR BIBLE

35 songs: At Seventeen • Blackbird • Fire and Rain • Happy Together • Leaving on a Jet Plane • Our House • Time in a Bottle • Turn! Turn! Turn! • You've Got a Friend • more.
00690464 .... $19.95

GRUNGE GUITAR BIBLE

30 songs: All Apologies • Counting Blue Cars • Glycerine • Jesus Christ Pose • Lithium • Man in the Box • Nearly Lost You • Smells like Teen Spirit • This Is a Call • Violet • and more.
00690649 .... $17.95

HARD ROCK GUITAR BIBLE

35 songs: Ballroom Blitz • Bang a Gong • Barracuda • Living After Midnight • Rock You like a Hurricane • School's Out • Welcome to the Jungle • You Give Love a Bad Name • more.
00690453 .... $19.95

INSTRUMENTAL GUITAR BIBLE

37 great instrumentals: Always with Me, Always with You • Green Onions • Hide Away • Jessica • Linus and Lucy • Perfidia • Satch Boogie • Tequila • Walk Don't Run • and more.
00690514 .... $19.95

JAZZ GUITAR BIBLE

31 songs: Body and Soul • In a Sentimental Mood • My Funny Valentine • Nuages • Satin Doll • So What • Star Dust • Take Five • Tangerine • Yardbird Suite • and more.
00690466 .... $19.95

MODERN ROCK GUITAR BIBLE

26 rock favorites: Aerials (System of a Down) • Alive (P.O.D.) • Cold Hard Bitch (Jet) • Kryptonite (3 Doors Down) • Like a Stone (Audioslave) • Whatever (Godsmack) • and more.
00690724 .... $19.95

NÜ METAL GUITAR BIBLE

25 edgy metal hits: Aenema • Black • Edgecrusher • Last Resort • People of the Sun • Schism • Southtown • Take a Look Around • Toxicity • Youth of the Nation • and more.
00690569 .... $19.95

POP/ROCK GUITAR BIBLE

35 pop hits: Change the World • Heartache Tonight • Money for Nothing • Mony, Mony • Pink Houses • Smooth • Summer of '69 • 3 AM • What I Like About You • and more.
00690517 .... $19.95

R&B GUITAR BIBLE

35 R&B classics: Brick House • Fire • I Got You (I Feel Good) • Love Rollercoaster • Shining Star • Sir Duke • Super Freak • and more.
00690452 .... $19.95

ROCK GUITAR BIBLE

33 songs: All Day and All of the Night • Born to Be Wild • Day Tripper • Hey Joe • Jailhouse Rock • Money • Paranoid • Sultans of Swing • Walk This Way • You Really Got Me • more!
00690313 .... $19.95

ROCKABILLY GUITAR BIBLE

31 songs from artists such as Elvis, Buddy Holly and the Brian Setzer Orchestra: Blue Suede Shoes • Hello Mary Lou • Peggy Sue • Rock This Town • Travelin' Man • and more.
00690570 .... $19.95

SOUL GUITAR BIBLE

33 songs: Groovin' • I've Been Loving You Too Long • Let's Get It On • My Girl • Respect • Theme from Shaft • Soul Man • and more.
00690506 .... $19.95

SOUTHERN ROCK GUITAR BIBLE

25 southern rock classics: Can't You See • Free Bird • Hold On Loosely • La Grange • Midnight Rider • Sweet Home Alabama • and more.
00690723 .... $19.95

Prices, contents, and availability subject to change without notice.

FOR MORE INFORMATION, SEE YOUR LOCAL MUSIC DEALER, OR WRITE TO:

HAL•LEONARD® **CORPORATION**
7777 W. BLUEMOUND RD. P.O. BOX 13819 MILWAUKEE, WI 53213

Visit Hal Leonard online at **www.halleonard.com**

0606